Forewo
Bestselling Aut

MW01706593

Press On!

Going Your Way No Matter What "They" May Say

How Naysayers Cause Us To Grow and Succeed

Michael Kerrigan
Author of the Innovative *What Choice Do I Have?*

A ***Possibility Press*** Book

Press On!

Michael Kerrigan

ISBN 978-0-938716-48-8

Published by
Possibility Press
PossibilityPress.com

Manufactured in the United States of America

Foreword

Press On Toward What YOU *Really* Want!

Pressing on in the face of rejection—Wow! That's the story of my life and it needs to be the story of yours as well, especially if it's important for you to live a great life! For it's only in pressing on that you can elevate yourself above the ordinary—and transcend the frustration of limits and rejection to a happier, more fulfilling life experience.

Jam-packed with wisdom, *Press On!* helps you deal with naysayers and others who would try to discourage you, take you off track, and hinder your progress. Pressing on toward your dream or objective—no matter what anyone else may think, say, or do—is the grandest adventure of life. It'll cause you to stretch, grow, and become all you were meant to be. Michael skillfully teaches you, using brilliant examples, how not to let others' agendas direct the course of your life.

Every successful person I know lives by the principles revealed in this ground-breaking book. Read it and you'll know what they know in identifying naysayers for what they are—dream-stealing, objective-thwarting individuals who really don't understand what's inside of you to do—*and move on.* Some may not even want you to get ahead—of them!

Read and apply this remarkable book's teachings and focus on what you want, not what "they"—whether in person or online—say you should or shouldn't be, do, or have. Be sure to check out *Chapter 22, The Voice of Cyberspace.* It's an up-to-the-minute discussion of the benefits and pitfalls of using the Internet for advice, covering how to deal with naysayers on line.

Now what are you waiting for? Put the pedal to the metal and…*press on!*

Toward your continued success,

John Fuhrman

Contents

Prologue

Ignore the Naysayers and *Press On!*

To let the wishes or attitudes of anyone else derail you, including naysayers in person, in the media, or over the Internet, is unconscionable—as well as a source of great sadness and regret.

Most of us, at some point in our lives, believed anything was possible. For example, when we were children our visions of the future were limitless. We pictured ourselves being a firefighter, basketball star, famous singer, admired leader, an inventor, a writer, or something else. There was no question in our minds that this was the role we would play. We believed anything was possible—freedom, wealth, travel, adventure, stardom. We were so convinced that, by the time we turned twenty-one, we just knew we would change the world.

But much to our chagrin, far too many of us have let others have their way with us when it wasn't in our best interest. Before we realized it, we found ourselves detoured from pressing on toward our objectives, letting our heartfelt desires fade into oblivion. We got lost and settled for the mundane everydayness of an ordinary life.

Like many, we may have been lured into an inappropriate people-pleasing trap. We unthinkingly acquiesced to naysayers and those whom we thought cared about us. Whenever they said we should or shouldn't be, do, or have something, we listened. Unfortunately, this kept us from growing and led to an increasing level of discontent. Sadly, we probably never even questioned it because this seemed to be the way life was for most everybody we knew—lackluster and unfulfilled.

We tried to cope with the pain by falling into bad habits like overeating, smoking, drinking, incessantly seeking entertainment and instant gratification, and by buying and doing things we couldn't afford. But none of these things worked; they only made matters worse. These attempts to compensate for a life not fully lived never led to happiness and success.

We became employees instead of business owners—second fiddle instead of conductor. We caved in to the seeds of doubt others planted in our minds. We got bogged down by doing what we thought we were *supposed* to do, rather than pressing on in our own direction—staying the course, going the distance. When we shared our aspirations, we were told we should just be thankful for what we have, we weren't being practical, or we were nothing more than dreamers.

We may even have been asked, "Who do you think you are?" The enlivened spirit of following the call to adventure, boldly meeting and overcoming challenges, and living the life we had once imagined no longer seemed so important.

We allowed naysayers to beat us up to where we ended up doing or not doing what they told us we should or shouldn't do—and we lost our way. Our vision of a brighter future may not have disappeared entirely, but it dimmed or went out of focus.

Continuing to do what others said was more important or more secure, our vision of the exciting life we had imagined got lost. Some of us even used the word should in our self-talk, as an excuse or permission not to grow and become happier and more successful. Life droned on as we gradually gave up the hope of having a better tomorrow. We had let one or more people discourage us. Our desires went into cardiac arrest and there was no one around to help us revive them. We put our tails between our legs, went home, shut down, and forgot about them.

But why?

Some people try to sabotage our desires, giving advice that only plants seeds of doubt—either personally or over the Internet. They really don't know us or the facts, nor do they truly care about what's on our hearts to do.

It seems that all of us have had episodes of giving up what we really wanted for what we were told were good, sensible reasons. Or we second-guessed ourselves out of a fear of failure, never even attempting to run for office, start a business, or follow through on an idea for an invention. We let the negative influence of others cause us to turn our backs on our objectives.

How sad....

Acquiescing to naysayers who use the innocent-sounding six-letter word, should (or shouldn't) is at least partly responsible for many of us not being where we'd like to be. Of course, where *you* are now may be just fine. But only you know for sure. You may already be doing what you really want to do with your life. If so, congratulations! But two out of three people *aren't*—largely because they gave in to the naysayers.

Rest assured, this book is not intended to teach that should can never be used. There are certainly situations where it is appropriate and desirable, which are discussed later. However, should is typically not well received. When people are told they should or shouldn't be, do, or have something, it tends to elicit a feeling of rebellion. They feel anger at some level but may not even be sure why. They stuff their feelings, while resentment eventually builds to where they lash out in unexpected ways.

Most people don't think about how the word should, when used inappropriately, can negatively affect relationships, life choices, and leadership effectiveness. This book addresses those issues, sharing how to press on no matter what the circumstances may be.

Manipulators often use should to further their own agendas at the expense of others. They are not concerned about creating win-win situations. Win-lose may be just fine with them. They use should or shouldn't to coerce and control, and often give advice without being qualified to do so. They attempt to maintain the status quo. Naysayers try to instill fear and don't want others to get ahead of them. They tend to be jealous and discount other people's desires. "Misery loves company" prevails.

Some people also use should or shouldn't to establish or maintain order. Consider the family structure you probably lived in from the day you were brought home from the hospital, until you went out on your own. Your parents and older siblings may have started wagging their fingers at you, lecturing about the way life is around the old homestead—*their* homestead.

The older the sibling, the more he or she may have felt entitled, or even responsible, to tell you how things should or shouldn't be. Most of the time, however, they didn't use those words per se. They were more prone to use the power-packed phrases, "You'd better...."; "You must…"; or "You better not…." They didn't want you thinking you had a choice.

The implications may have been serious—if you did or didn't do what they said, you would be in BIG trouble! Childhood sibling relationships are only one example. Then, as adults, they often continue the habit of trying to establish or maintain control in dealing with others.

With the lingering unease you may have experienced from those encounters, you might have settled for many of the mediocre relationships you have today. Now that you've decided to press on and are, perhaps, associating with more positive people, you may be aware of undercurrents of dissatisfaction with some of your previously developed relationships. While you may have been doing your best to ignore those feelings, they are still there—that's understandable. Your siblings, as well as many of your long-time friends and acquaintances, may have chosen to maintain the status quo while you've chosen to move on. Think about it. Are you still friends with everyone you knew in school or college? There just isn't enough time to maintain quality relationships where there's now less in common.

Millions of people have experienced the consequences of following naysayers' advice. You're hardly alone! We often use the negative messages we received and adhered to when we were growing up to guide us in our current decisions and activities—appropriately or not. How often have you done what you thought was expected of you, and stayed precisely where you were, happy or not? Acquiescing to naysayers boxes us in and holds us back.

And there we stay—*stuck!*

What if the Wright brothers had given in to those who said they should just continue building and repairing bicycles? What if they had bought into the conventional wisdom of the 1890s that said "If God had intended man to fly, he would have given us wings"? Today, the aviation and aerospace industries account for more than ten percent of the economy in the United States alone. Where would we be today if the Wrights had given in to naysayers? Where would we be today if all the innovators and business-minded people had surrendered to those who advocated the status quo of "We should be satisfied with where we are and with what we have"?

You've chosen to read this book because you're moving ahead. At stake is the realization of your potential, but only if you reach for it. You've gotten to the point where you're ready to move on from the constraints of the naysayers. You can now devote a larger part of your time and energy toward following through with more of your own choices. Challenging the inappropriate dictates of others will help you press on, while your example will encourage others to do the same. Dealing firmly yet kindly with those who would try to have you submit to their negativity can help you do what may now seem impossible.

Remember, naysayers can give advice based only on *their* perspectives and desires, not yours. They simply don't know what's inside of you. This book will help you deal more effectively with others and their opinions while you go forward, doing what's best for you. You'll be clearer about and more committed to doing what's on your heart and encouraged to press on. After all, it's *your* objective; not theirs. They probably think they couldn't follow it themselves anyway. Or, perhaps, they're jealous that you're spending time on your positive new agenda and that you'll grow beyond them.

> *"I cannot give you the formula for success, but I can give you the formula for failure—try to please everybody."*
>
> —Herbert Bayard Swope

Apply what you learn in this book and you'll grow stronger in dealing with naysayers and their agendas. They'll no longer be able to stop or slow you down from pressing on toward greater happiness and success, and whatever you're striving for. You'll be making more decisions and taking more actions that are best for *you!*

Your vision of a brighter future, born of desire and faith, is the guidepost to pressing on. No matter how much the naysayers try to prevent you from moving on, stay the course. Muster the courage to awaken even the whisper of a dream. Cling to what you know is best for you and your family, and rely on those who support you.

Acquiescing to inappropriate naysaying compromises your better judgment and can ruin your life, which is far too precious not to live as you envision. Now is the time, once and for all, to discount the opinions of those who may be holding you back. Press on with a new sense of urgency. No matter what *"they"* may think, say, or do in their attempts to stop you from doing so, ignore their negativity and hold on tight to your objective. Go forward in faith and create the life you want.

Press on,

Michael Kerrigan

1

A *Good* Reason Is Hard to Find

There's a fine line between caring and controlling. Make sure people aren't stepping over that line in their efforts to seemingly watch out for your best interest.

Naysaying comes from just about everywhere, including parents, siblings, friends, bosses, co-workers, associates, the Internet, spouses, city ordinances, and even kids. They all try to control or manipulate us with varying degrees of success.

In their efforts to lord over us, some use guilt while others use fear. Still others rely on saying "It's your civic duty" to get you to act in certain ways, based on *their* agendas. They say you should keep your nose to the grindstone, or tell you not to try anything new. These shoulds are intended to do two things: a) control your behavior and b) make life easier—*for them.*

We even generate shoulds for ourselves! A big one for many people is, just be happy with the way things are and forget about my dreams. Notice the difference between being influenced by good and reasonable ideas, versus being controlled by guilt and an assortment of other emotion-packed directives. The difference is that guilt-charged shoulds are likely to leave you feeling angry, frustrated, or afraid.

Whether shoulds come from you or someone else, learn to recognize them when they appear. Tuning out should is the first step in dealing with it effectively. Put it where it belongs—outside your new world of reason. Don't let should interfere with your desire to do and be the best for yourself and your family.

Enter the Ever-Present Authority Figures

Parents, teachers, bosses, and institutions, and a variety of others believe they need to direct you in one way or another—way beyond their role or responsibility.

Many parents take their cue from something quite basic—the wild. For example, a mother tiger nuzzles her cub this way and that, teaching it to feed, play, hunt, and do the things that tigers do. After all, the cub will need those skills to survive once it's away from its mother's caring supervision. For wild animals in their natural environment, this is the way it needs to be.

In the wild, an animal's options are limited. When it gets hungry, it better know how to hunt, or else. A tiger cub doesn't have the option of choosing between getting a quick bite at the corner restaurant, popping a frozen dinner in the microwave, or going to the local burger house for a mega meal.

For every learned or imitative behavior a tiger cub has, we, as discerning human beings, have one or more options. For every task an animal instinctively performs, we humans have choices. Always doing certain things in exactly the same way makes sense—but only if you're an animal in the wild. There, shoulds play a big role.

We've all had our experiences with parents, or other caretakers, who act like protective mother tigers. They gave us should orders because they believed that would keep us safe, educated, liked, and, of course, germ-free. Remember being told you should—wash your hands, say thank you, and kiss Grandma goodbye? Parents want to keep their children in line with shoulds so they can live an error-less, pain-free life, and survive with minimal discomfort.

Parental advice is good, but there's a limit. If we weren't given some direction as youngsters, we might act like cats in the wild, carrying small rodents around in our mouths! But we grew up and moved out of the house a long time ago. Even so that hasn't prevented parents from picking up the phone and telling their adult kids to, essentially, wipe their noses! There's a fine line between caring and controlling. Make sure people aren't stepping over that line in their efforts to seemingly watch out for your best interests.

Now parents certainly aren't alone in issuing should orders and making should rules; teachers fall into the same trap. When you sat down in Mrs. Hollybush's class to learn algebra, she had a good reason to include should with her instructions. Solving an equation for "x" should be done by using a few specific steps, or else you simply won't get the right answer. Sure, you can guess. But guessing won't get you where you need to go. Furthermore, when you're directed to show your work, guessing is generally a red flag that you haven't a clue about what you're doing.

Once you wander into the world of the social sciences, things are a little less clear—more subject to viewpoints. For example, political science isn't math. In the world of the softer sciences, shoulds are almost always met with at least one side believing you shouldn't! For every group that says we should build a dam, there's another that says the river should run free. So who's right? The answer isn't nearly as clear as solving for "x." But making a decision together through considerate brainstorming, rather than accepting other shoulds, often produces the most beneficial solution.

It's the Law!

Institutions are right behind parents and teachers in dispensing shoulds. Actually, they are probably the worst offenders when it comes to using shoulds as their guiding lights. Rather than helping you grow to adulthood or pass the ninth grade, institutions aren't nearly so helpful or concerned. Shoulds, in their hands, have a more grating purpose. They're used to getting you to *conform.*

The expansion of Interstate 25 through the heart of Denver is a great example. This project, dubbed T-REX (yes, as in the unruly dinosaur), was originally scheduled to take four to seven years to complete. And by all accounts, it promised to be a noisy project as it jostled people living on both sides of the 19-mile stretch of unrelenting construction.

The time frame was a little vague because before any construction comes destruction—lots of it. In part, 12 old bridges spanning the highway had to be replaced. Here's what the state and the contractor told the affected residents: You should let us make a lot of noise 24 hours a day, especially during bridge replacement time. After all, it's for a good cause!

The reason for the project's vague timeline finally surfaces. If the demolition of the bridges is allowed to be carried out (loudly), even during normal sleeping hours, the project will take only four years. Otherwise, it could well take the full seven years. Fortunately, bridge demolition will be done in short segments and only at the front end of the project. And while it won't be at the noise-level of passenger jets taking off every minute for four years, people will definitely lose some sleep.

So, should people go along with what the sponsors of the project are proposing as the prudent thing to do? After all, the sponsors are pretty sure they know what's best. But not everyone agrees. Some opposing the project are simply not willing to do what they're being told they should. So are *they* right? Who knows? But at least they're aware of their options, rather than blindly following when shoulds are being thrown their way. Some people aren't willing to play a predictable, acquiesce-to-should, passive role. And, of course, it's these people who lead the pack of those less vocal in their opposition.

The institutional approach of using shoulds is *duty*-based—as in "it's *your* duty." It's designed to encourage obedience to help the institution meet its deadlines and save costs while sacrificing the comfort of only a few for the supposed best interest of the many. As for the institution, the *many* is what's important. But what about you? Frankly, the institution doesn't really care. It has its own politically influenced agenda.

Yes Sir, Yes Ma'am?

Everyone has his or her own preferences, priorities, wants, and needs. So how often will someone else's priority be yours—especially when that someone else is the boss or has been designated as being in charge? This brings us to dealing with those who are calling the shots. They often throw their weight around—in some cases, just to flaunt the power they have in the position they've been given.

Everyone has had a boss at one time or another. When some start working, this person is often either the head burger flipper or the assistant shift manager. Typically, they are fairly focused as they go about issuing orders: "Get those fries out of that fat!" And the fries come out. If the employees to whom the orders are barked disobey, the boss knows there are always plenty of others who can replace them. (Have you noticed how some employers always seem to have a "Now Hiring" sign in the window?)

Most of us, unless we are self-employed, have to take orders from other sorts of bosses. We may even end up answering to someone who is supposed to be more skilled than the assistant shift manager. And how do we know that? They use shoulds! "Get those fries out of that fat!" becomes "You should get those fries out of that fat!" See the difference? They may sound a bit better and less authority-wielding but, as mentioned earlier, shoulds tend to build resentment.

Of course, good bosses are more sophisticated than that—especially those who reach management's upper levels. As far as they're concerned, shoulds have a much higher purpose: to meet deadlines, increase the bottom line and, *always,* to control. (Note: From the finance-driven perspective, the scale of the project and the money involved are the only things that really separate "fries" from other, "higher" callings.) It happens in every business and industry, from the best-intended non-profit organizations to the largest corporations: should tends to have free rein. And it's not good!

Going Off Automatic

Now the intent here isn't to get you to turn a deaf ear to should—especially when your boss is serious, which most of them tend to be. That would be irresponsible. The trick here is to truly listen to what's being said and decide whether it *really* makes the best sense. You'll ultimately have more control and get greater respect from others. Here's an example of how it could work:

Your boss, Mr. Burns, thinks you should pay a visit to the water bladder manufacturing plant in East Aardvark because sales are down 15 percent from last year. "Check it out," Mr. Burns says.

As you reflect upon it with your increased awareness of how should is used, you realize Mr. Burns tends to give out orders seemingly at random. He also disregards any scheduled time off he may have already agreed to give you before he barks out the new orders. You, like most employees, have always said yes to his orders—without thinking. As a result, you have disappointed your wife, your kids, and others, many times in the past because you gave in to Burns's shoulds.

This time, however, you analyze Burns's orders so you can determine their true meaning. Not only is this the right thing to do, but Burns's new directive conflicts with plans you've already made and he's already approved. The truth is that you have a business you're developing. You and your wife had planned to spend the next two days at a related convention. The new directive is creating conflicts on a variety of fronts: nonrefundable airline tickets, new information that will come out of the convention, contacts you would undoubtedly make and, of course, your wife's expectations of going—*with* you. Are you really going to let Burns have his way with you once more?

In a lot of cases, people receiving this order do what they were told without a second thought. They would do what they had always done before, regardless of any previous plans or the wisdom of the order itself. They'd fly out to East Aardvark International Airport first thing Monday morning, tour the plant, grill the production supervisor, visit the water bladder manufacturing operation, kick the tires of the big rigs down at the loading dock, and report *something* back to Burns. And why not? This is what they were told they should do. So they just do it!

Another thing to consider when analyzing this should is whether it is what Burns or any other boss really wants. Does he or they want someone who follows orders without thinking? In some cases, the boss may be too insecure to confidently receive feedback from one of his or her employees. But let's say, for example, Burns isn't insecure. Sure, he told you to check it out; but Burns has twelve things floating around in his head, and he was just speaking in shorthand. His concern (and that of *his* boss) is *really* about declining sales. Does this mean a trip to the manufacturing plant is necessarily the company's best first move? Probably not.

Now, it's time to take yourself out of automatic mode and consider more seriously the waning patience of your loving wife. You figure that you could probably get a lot more relevant information from the marketing department. At least it's a good place to start. If it's a problem with bladder quality, then a trip to the plant might be in order. If it's a challenge because the water bladder market is saturated, then the difficulty might reside in advertising or sales. Or maybe it's simply something beyond your control. One thing is certain though: Kicking truck tires at the loading dock isn't going to change the way prospective buyers look at water bladders.

The truly responsible thing to do, both as a professional and a loving husband, is to listen to and think about the should-order being given, consider the alternatives, and then act in a kind, measured, and reasonable way. As you listen and respond *appropriately*, several positive things begin to happen, including increased self-respect, regardless of how spontaneous or reasoned the order may have been.

When you listen to shoulds with empathy and understanding, and don't automatically say yes just to please the boss in the short-run, you'll more clearly perceive the assignment's importance and its meaning as well as your personal situation. You'll be able to assign specific values to the direction being given, the information the boss really needs, and the previous personal commitment you made. When you look at it all from the broader perspective, you'll be of more benefit to the boss as well as to yourself and your wife.

You might be saying that this is a communications issue. You're absolutely right. That is precisely what should is all about: communicating an idea with an authoritative, six-letter word, or one of its cousins, in an attempt to manipulate an instant yes. But how *you* respond is under *your* control, no one else's. You might ask Mr. Burns: "Is a trip to East Aardvark really what we need and, if so, can it wait until next week? I've prepaid for a weekend trip with my wife, and I'll really be in trouble if I tell her I've got to work." It could be as simple as that! Just be open and honest.

2

Do Your Peers *Really* Know What's Best for YOU?

Regardless of how you see them, some people will think of you as a peer and hand out shoulds based on that assumption.

There are people who believe it's not only their right, but also their responsibility, to tell you how you *should* be doing things. They share this information because it makes them appear to be bright, caring, and on top of things. Without invitation, they are quite happy with this role. They are your *peers*.

Not everyone thinks of peers in the same way. Some believe they are people who live in the same neighborhood—similar houses, similar cars, similar kids—with slightly different situations and hair colors. Others think peers are those who line up with them on an organizational chart at work. "Yeah, there's Bob. He's a second-assistant, junior mid-level manager on the way up, just like me. He's a peer." Still others think they don't have any peers at all—they believe they are on a level all by themselves. But no matter how anyone considers peers, should is often used by those who are just jealous of them or not as bright as *they* are.

We all like thinking we're special—and we all are, in our own ways. Even so, no one is a big deal. We all have skills and roles to play. However, as part of the human race, we do share some similarities. From someone's perspective, we all fit (or are *put*) into various categories. Just look at the U.S. census: over 300 million people stuck into fourteen convenient racial categories, further defined by income, geographical area, profession, and so on.

It's easy to pigeonhole people and believe that everyone you want to cram into that hole is the same. So somewhere resides a peer group. That's easy to understand. But regardless of how you may see *them*, some people will see *you* as a peer and dispense shoulds based on that assumption.

For those of us who are altruistic in nature, the feel-good of helping someone who says we should might be enough. But most of us are steeped in a life we aren't too crazy about. We need to be focusing on helping others in order to better our lives. Getting a feel-good isn't quite enough.

Generally, anyone who wants something—and will manipulate you into helping him or her get it—doesn't go into any detail about why you should do it. When he or she doesn't give a reason, the true agenda isn't exposed. The risk of rejection is minimized.

That individual probably stands a 50 percent chance of getting people to go along with the idea that they should because of most people's programmed compliant nature. This guarantees a higher success rate than if the manipulator were to actually explain the manipulative scheme and selfish motive.

Peers are also found in families as siblings, neighbors, friendly competitors with whom you've shared bowling lanes over the past twenty years, and others. At one time or another, they've all undoubtedly directed the word should at you—and *meant* it: "You should call Mom," "You should get that lawn mowed," "You should just work your job and be satisfied with what you have,"

"You should straighten your wrist out when you release the ball." Guilt, conformity, *and* control is their basic mode of operation.

Be Faithful to Your Own Priorities

In the short-run, it's easier to say yes to should and please the *should*er. And that's fine, if you don't have other priorities that are important to you, your family, your business, or career. It's okay to please others, unless it hurts you and your objective.

The implication of saying no is subject to interpretation, in this case their *worst* interpretation—that you've rejected the *should*er. What might saying no mean to a friend who supposedly cares about you and hopefully respects your priorities?

Remember, saying "Let me think about it" just delays the inevitable call back. So what do you do?

Even though your day may be planned from beginning to end, you may still be tempted to drop everything you're doing, say yes, and do something off track. That may allow you to remain a part of a group you participated with in the past—not because you care but to maintain the status quo. This is inappropriate people pleasing at its worst, and far too many of us do it far too often.

This "Well, okay" attitude is responsible for aunts, uncles, grandfathers, and great grandmothers who didn't reach *their* potential because of what *others* thought *they* should do. They allowed should to incessantly get in the way of what *they* wanted to do too. Is that how you want to live your life? Are naysaying *should*ers happy people and good examples of what you want to be?

Do what you need to do to be faithful to your priorities. It's the only way you'll truly win in life. Be courageous enough to say no, as necessary, rather than just go along with the should crowd.

Someday Becomes a New Word Called *Never!*

There are others who are more than delighted to tell you what you should be doing in terms of charity. The words should, time, and money always seem to appear in the same sentence, never more than a breath away from the word giving. This is not to say there aren't legitimate charities or causes. There are hundreds of organizations doing great works for those in need.

Unfortunately, those who volunteer for these organizations may be doing so without first putting their own financial houses in order. They may be "putting the cart before the horse," as the saying goes. They erroneously believe that volunteering for some so-called greater good relieves them of their own personal responsibility.

They think that giving in to should will relieve their pain. They're probably in debt, and would be better off improving their financial situation instead of volunteering. Once they've gained financial freedom, they could volunteer all the time and money they want to. That would be noble, but first things first—priorities, priorities.

In addition to the possibility that participating in *their* mission may not be related to your objective or keep you on it, there are others whose sole purpose is to get some of your money. They operate as telemarketers, infomercial presenters, door-to-door solicitors, and in dozens of other guises—all designed to pull at your heart strings and get you to respond as they think you should. It's not that all such organizations or individuals in these arenas are of the take-unfair-advantage-of-others mindset. Like anything else, there are good and not-so-good people involved.

How *you* choose to respond to any of these causes or pleas is entirely up to you. But don't be afraid to say "No!" if it's something that could deter you from pressing on. Just be aware that there are some ill-intentioned people out there. They often reveal their unkind attitudes by being inconsiderate and fast talking. They are conveniently deaf when it comes to hearing "No," or "Sorry, I'm not interested," continuing to talk as if you said nothing. If they're incredibly rude and obnoxious and won't stop badgering you, it might be best to just hang up. Use your own judgment.

In many of these cases, your yielding to their will only causes you to set your own best interests aside. By doing so, you ignore *your own* wants and needs and stray off course.

> *By its very nature, a dream—even one that's barely alive—is a very precious thing. To make it a reality, you need to make it a priority—a beautiful, clear objective that you simply must achieve. You just have to do it or you feel your life won't be complete or even worthwhile.*

So what can happen to you if you lose your way? How can a dream lose its heartbeat and fade into oblivion—never to be thought of except, perhaps, on occasion? With so many people bidding for your time, money, and attention, it's all too easy to be lured off track and let the dream slide, or put it on hold for the time being. To achieve what you really want, you need to focus on it with all the strength you can muster. Putting your dream on hold to inappropriately please someone else can be the beginning of the end—*someday* becomes a new word called *never.*

3

Putting Your Emotions Into Perspective

Even when people are railing at you to behave in certain ways and do specific things, how you respond is up to you.

There are two things that can affect whether or not you let down your guard and give in to the *should*ers—guilt and ambiguity. Here are some practical ways to deal with them.

Employing guilt to elicit action is well recognized, practiced, and abused. Why? Because it's so *effective*. Virtually everyone responds to it. Here are a few examples:

- You work overtime, get a second job, or build a business to increase your income and better support your family; and others criticize you for being away from your children.
- Fundraisers look at not-yet-full donation jars and send them around for another pass; and guilt prompts wallets and purses to open wide.
- Officemates who are still working give you forlorn looks when you pick up your briefcase—long after 5 p.m.—and head for the door; and you still feel like a slacker.

Yes, guilt often gets results. However, if you find yourself feeling manipulated—where guilt and should go hand in hand—there are things you can do to put guilt in its place. Ask yourself these questions:

- Why would I be concerned?
- How responsible am I for the situation?
- What additional information do I need to properly evaluate this request?
- Do I need more time (a day, a week, or a month) to reasonably evaluate this request?
- Am I already doing something about it?

Why would I be concerned? We're all busy. Chances are your job, family, various associations constantly bid for your attention. But it's up to you, with your priorities firmly in mind, how to respond. There may also be other aspects of your life over which you can exercise more control, for example, by saying "No!" as appropriate. You obviously have some influence, or others wouldn't look to you for leadership, decisions, or action.

But what do you do when something erupts outside of what you consider normal? What do you do when someone approaches you and says, "You should help," "You should pay," or "You should be concerned"?

It may seem a little out of character, initially, but your first question to yourself might best be "Why?"

Answering this enables you to start putting the request into perspective, and helps you decide if any more thought about it is even warranted. Responding is up to you. If it's obviously something that could get you off track, then even bothering to answer the question is waste of time. But at least asking *why* helps reinforce that you do have choices and, perhaps, you can define what they are.

How responsible am I? Most of us are responsible enough to jump into action when one of our interests is involved or threatened, and it's almost instinctive to defend a friend or lend a hand if a catastrophe strikes someone we love.

Fortunately, episodes requiring focused, heartfelt efforts are rare. Even *one* crisis, though, can temporarily drain our resources—from our emotions to our wallets—before we can regroup and get back on track to our goal.

Of course, there are those who deal with other people's crises every day: police, firefighters, emergency room doctors and nurses, and the like. However, if you aren't being paid to do so, it's prudent to consider if the emergency is something with which you really need to be involved.

Asking yourself, "How responsible am I for the situation?" will help give you some perspective on your need to get involved, and how deep and time-consuming that involvement needs to be.

What additional information do I need to properly evaluate this request? Act like a reporter on a fact-finding mission. A series of questions needs to be answered before a reporter can begin to fairly evaluate a story's value and potential reader interest. He or she needs answers to who, what, when, where, why, and how, as well as *additional* questions, before sitting down to write a decent story. These questions may sound a lot like: "What were you thinking when you...?" This takes the story a lot farther than the simple question "What happened?"

When you're approached with should, first find out what's *really* going on. Get this answered before you get caught up enough to potentially intervene and take direct action. Finding out all you can before you choose whether or not to get involved, at whatever level, will save you a lot of headaches and hurt feelings later on.

Do I need more time (a day, week, or a month) to reasonably evaluate this request? The short answer is yes. If you even consider the question, and feel like you need to take at least a deep breath, you are probably being pressured to do *something*! Giving in under the influence of charged emotions and only a few facts can be one of the most counterproductive things you can do.

About a year ago, Fred, a friend of mine, received an e-mail from Jan, a business associate, that was tart in tone and pointed in its allegations. She accused Fred of neglecting one of their clients, who was threatening to pull his business because Fred wasn't keeping them informed.

"We'll see," Fred thought angrily. And, without giving himself a chance to cool off, he fired back his own aggressive response to Jan. I won't go into all the ugly details, but Fred wrote, essentially, that the client was lazy, hadn't bothered to read Fred's reports, and that Jan really was out of her league in second-guessing the approach Fred was taking with the account. As Fred typed in his name and triumphantly hit send, he noticed that he had also inadvertently sent a copy to the client.

Would taking a deep breath have helped? You bet. Waiting a few hours, or even a day or more, to respond thoughtfully to Jan's e-mail, could have helped save the account, or at least have allowed a window of time for him to think it through and suggest how the account might be restructured. There was no good reason to rush the response. Sure, Fred needed to get involved. But waiting until he was in *a better frame of mind* would have helped—a lot.

Am I already doing something about it?

> *People with big hearts often take action when they're asked or are told they should. "What can I do?" is often the first thing to come out of their mouths. If this reaction isn't held in check, though, these kindhearted souls tend to lose focus on pressing on in deference to inappropriately pleasing others.*

But right behind the rush to someone's aid is the vague, head-cocking thought that this situation sounds *familiar*. "Oh, yeah," he or she will think, "I'm already contributing to Helpful Way or United Hands" or any one of a number of quality service groups. "Don't *they* cover this?"

Once you establish that you are already doing something for this cause, ask yourself this: "Do I need to get more involved or am I doing quite enough as it is?" When should makes an appearance, ask yourself: "Do I already have this base *covered*?"

One additional step you can take to put guilt-ladling into perspective is to find out who else is involved in helping. If you absolutely believe you must do something, consider sharing the responsibility in a way that doesn't get you off track to the dream or goal you are, or want to be, pursuing.

Find out how much of *their* time and resources the demanders are contributing to the cause. You are about to be taken unfair advantage of if you're asked to take on the responsibility alone, although they may work hard at attempting to persuade you that you should.

When former U.S. Secretary of State Colin Powell visited the Middle East early in the Bush administration, he said political maneuvering and standoffs had to change. The involvement of the United States in efforts to bring about peace would take a back seat. The principals—the Israelis and Palestinians—would have to do the coordinating, talking, and compromising. And then, at the point of agreement, the U.S. government would step in and assist in executing an agreement. "We cannot want peace more than you want it for yourselves," Powell said.

So it is in dealing with those who are telling you how to behave: Allowing yourself to be cajoled into a position—one you may be somewhat skeptical of in the first place—is doomed to frustration and probable failure.

Once responsibility sharing is in place, *follow up in a positive way*. Tracking how an effort is going isn't being nosey. Hold people accountable for their actions, so you can avoid making mistakes or supporting efforts that are going nowhere.

Getting a Clear Picture

In my first book, *What Choice Do I Have?,* I shared: "Because there are no guarantees of success, people tend to assume the absolute worst will happen when they make a move or change some behavior. This outlook of defeat is triggered by ambiguity."

This *can* be one of your most aggressive enemies if you operate under the order of should. When you don't know specifically what you'll be doing and how, ambiguity can take over and cause you to drift aimlessly.

> *What will happen if I don't act as I'm told I should? Don't ask the* shoulder*—ask yourself. The next time someone says you should do what* they *want, stick with* your *priorities. Trust the instinct that tells you not to act and picture how beautifully the situation will turn out without your help.*

Monitor the situation for a week, a month, or a year—however long it takes for it to play itself out. See if the actual outcome is even close to the other person's predictions of doom. Then look at the consequences of your decision: Could you have had a positive influence on the outcome and would it have been good for you, or was this just another attempt to manipulate you?

Even when people are railing at you to behave in certain ways and do specific things, your response is up to you. It is your prerogative to change your habitual yes responses. You owe it to yourself and those you care about to carefully consider whether or not to respond with yeses to shoulds from others. Look ahead and thoughtfully decide what is yours to do and what responsibilities belong to others. It'll help you determine your future and the role you'll play in it.

4

The "I"s Have It

We can fairly well anticipate the consequences of our actions or what will happen if we don't *act—if we* don't *go for that promotion or build our business and press on in our own chosen direction.*

Once you filter out the *should*ers of the world—the bosses, the peers, the demanders, and the requesters—you have only one more to deal with: *you*! Yes, oftentimes we have only ourselves to blame for the ultimatums we deliver or accept.

"I should…" is a phrase each of us has muttered to ourselves at some point: "I should have said...", "I should have gone…", "I should have remembered…", or "I should have done…". What everyone else is capable of doing to us—if we allow it—we are also capable of doing to ourselves!

If you go down the road of detrimental self-instruction, you'll begin to script your behavior in ways you may later regret. You tell yourself how you should behave, even when that behavior may not be to your advantage. You tell yourself what to believe, even if those beliefs are contrary to what you know is best for you.

Scripts are made up of that internal dialogue you rely on to get from one activity, place, point, or relationship to the next. When it is laden with shoulds, you are left with just one way to go, one way to behave in any particular situation. Choices seem to disappear. You limit your options when you operate under the influence of should.

Far too often, these scripts—which reflect the nature of our self-talk—are negative and damaging when they're loaded with the command of "I should." Let's take a few minutes to look at the way you are treating yourself with your self-talk.

- When was the last time you said "I should"?
- What were you thinking of doing?
- If you did take action, what was the outcome?

Looking at this a different way, if you were telling yourself you should have behaved differently:

- What were you regretting that you had already done?
- Why did you behave that way in the first place?
- Why weren't you able to stop yourself before you acted?

This last trio of questions brings up a perspective that each of us deals with regularly—hindsight! It is truly a gift to be able to look back and gauge where we've been and determine the value of the actions that got us there. The only question is, why can't we do that before we act—before we make the mistake or let should run our lives and get us off track?

We can be logical. Within reason, we can fairly well anticipate the consequences of our actions or what will happen if we don't act—if we don't go for that promotion or build our business and press on in our own chosen direction. We know that inaction would only lead to disappointment.

Think About It!

Unfortunately, many people fail to invest time to really think. It can be a challenge to stop long enough to seriously think about what we're doing. We're all pulled in so many different directions that finding some peace and quiet to reason things out almost seems like a luxury—but in truth, it's a necessity. Anyone who is set on making his or her life better needs to stop, think, and plan.

Even when we're thinking thoughts that can brighten our future, we may get distracted by something—like a maintenance-type activity that we "should" be doing. We might lose sight of career or business-building activities that could help us enhance our future.

Again, take a few minutes and look at how you're responding to the shoulds that may be distracting you. This can shed some light on your past behaviors and help lay the groundwork for more constructive actions in the future. It can also have a significant impact on how quickly and directly you achieve the outcomes you want—the goals that, day by day, translate into the fruition of your dreams and objectives. It all centers on what you tell yourself and what you do as a result.

When you tell yourself you should be doing something you currently aren't doing, ask yourself these five questions:

- Is implementing the idea in my best interest?
- What's the motive behind it?
- What's the anticipated outcome?
- Who will be impacted?
- What's most likely going to happen?

Is implementing the idea in my best interest? Regardless of whose idea it may be, especially if it's presented in the form of should (or shouldn't), ask yourself if acting on it would take you off track. If the idea could deter you from pressing on, reject it immediately. Stop it in its tracks before it stops you in yours.

Take the time to think about ideas so you can make quality decisions before you decide whether or not to take action. Robotically taking action without thinking, just because someone says you should or shouldn't, can take you off track.

What's the motive behind it? Ask yourself why this idea even came up. Why would something like this even have been proposed?

> *When we're* shoulding *ourselves—a close kin to kidding ourselves—we may feel justified in doing just about anything. "Yep," we say to ourselves, "I've been working hard. I think I should buy that expensive red sportscar. I'll just get a seven-year loan, so I can make the payments. But this is how many people go broke.*

We're all motivated to do all sorts of things for a variety of reasons—some good, some bad. So the next time you find yourself thinking you should be driving that expensive red sports car you really can't afford yet, ask yourself this: What's my motive? What am I trying to accomplish? Will it support or distract from my objective? Is it in keeping with my overall plan or vision?

What's the anticipated outcome? Take a look down the road. Do you like what you see when the idea becomes reality? Can you honestly embrace and live with all the aspects of the outcome you visualize? Or when you look into the future, does the outcome look more like a nightmare? Nightmares can come true, too, and are often the result of a series of unwise decisions that were acted upon.

We're all familiar with that high school science course that discussed cause and effect—for every action there is an equal and opposite reaction. Take a specific action and you can expect a certain result. For example, if you consistently eat too much food, you'll become overweight, not feel good, and ruin your health.

While relationships aren't as exact as the sciences, the same general rule applies. Take a specific course of action and you can generally anticipate a certain response. When you tell yourself you really should be doing something and know it isn't the best course of action, you're probably starting an unwelcome chain of events.

Who will be impacted by this action? When we tell ourselves we should be doing one thing or another, there are typically two recipients of the resulting action: ourselves and someone else. We need to ask ourselves who's going to be affected by this? If the action is to benefit you and, perhaps, your family, and that's your intent, then acting on your own is reasonable—even if others disagree. But why would you want to have a positive impact on someone, when all that's going to happen if you take a certain action is damaging to you?

There are lots of ways you can look at how you or others will be impacted. So honest answers, as well as appropriate action, will take you a long way toward the result you want. There's a lot of incentive to think in these terms, especially when you, and possibly your family, are involved—and will be living with the results you create.

What's really going to happen? Most of us wrestle with what we want to be in life, how we want to affect others, and our objectives. Some stay stuck just thinking about doing certain things. They spend too much time thinking and not enough time doing. Their procrastination leads to regret and a life not fully lived.

If we do things in response to should without thinking, we set in motion a series of actions that probably won't give us what we want. Going forward with the intention of sticking to your priorities is the best thing you can do. One way or the other, you're going to get results. If you're tired of the results you've been getting, you're probably not pressing on toward your own objectives. Motivate yourself to do what you know you need to do by focusing on your dream. To accomplish something different, you need to *do* something different!

Mentally tracing the course of your intention, from the germ of an idea through implementation to its most likely end, helps you create the best possible outcome. It will also help erase the doubt and arguing you've done with yourself over what you need to do.

Who's in Charge?—*Don't Ask Alice!*

Now you may be thinking, "Hey, *I should* works for me. I've got a good job and I'm focused. I know where I'm headed."

You're right—to a degree. *I should* sets a definite course—but it's typically based on the expectations of others, as is often found in the corporate environment. It discourages you from thinking about *your* plan. It locks you in to behaviors that may be directly in conflict with what you say *you* want. If your initial plan is truly your best plan, that's great—provided nothing changes as you proceed—as long as you can continue pressing on along a well-understood, unchanging course with no unexpected shifts. But life usually doesn't work that way. There are such things as lay-offs, downsizings, mergers, bankruptcies, and foreclosures. You need to be pressing on toward creating the life *you* want.

How often does a single-minded, rigid approach, like the typical 40-year career, allow you to meet new demands, especially if someone else is in charge? How could should possibly help you pursue your own objective when someone else is always telling you what to do! More importantly, is the chiseled-in-stone, rigid approach to living, working, and behaving the one *you* desire?

Consider Alice, the nicest person you would ever want to meet. Raised in Georgia, her manners are a holdover from that genteel southern era. It was a time when people asked about every living relative, remembered how pretty the apple blossoms were in the spring, and ended with an offer of lemonade? Alice goes out of her way to greet everyone she knows in this quaint, warm way.

She even acts this way to people who aren't crazy about her. "Because," Alice explains, "that's just the way I was raised. That's what I should do."

Unfortunately, not everyone is so warm in return. Alice even gets a little resistance as she plies her greeting to people who refuse to be charmed. Occasionally, it's even painful to watch. Alice hangs in there, though, refusing to abandon her script. She's not selective in how she deals with others, maintaining that everyone should be treated the same. Should rules her life; therefore, she alienates certain people.

As much as we may like to think we're in charge, other people and their priorities can get in the way. We need to be flexible enough to work around this so we can stay on track. Forcing yourself to perform just under *I should* usually ends in disappointment.

Life is a lot better when you're pressing on in your own direction, rather than giving in to innocent-sounding shoulds. Begin evaluating how you're programming yourself by asking one question: What kind of shoulds am I giving myself that aren't getting me what I want and need? Have I boxed myself into a life I don't like anymore?

If you're having a challenge thinking of something you're telling yourself you should do, think of some of the should statements you may be passing on to others—your spouse, kids, a co-worker, an associate, or an employee. Wouldn't it be better to completely abandon the should directive and communicate in a more agreeable way? Yes! Your relationships and your life will get better.

Your Personal Philosophy Is the Foundation

The first step toward creating some viable options to should is to examine your personal philosophy of life. This will give you a starting point in dealing with yourself and others. To begin with, being aware of what's truly acceptable to you and what's not will help you gain clarity and focus on the best options available to you—as well as the options you can give to others.

Make a conscious, courageous decision about how you really want to live your life. Ask yourself what's important to you personally, professionally, and emotionally, and write it down. Determine what kind of person you're choosing to be, and how you're choosing to interact most effectively and compassionately, both with yourself and others.

A personal philosophy can be as simple as a few words or a sentence. It may be as simple as: I treat myself with greater respect and continually work on gaining a greater understanding of others. I'm a person of integrity and compassion, always striving to do my best, and I make decisions that give me peace of mind.

Now, determine if the shoulds you're dealing with are consistent with the philosophy you're choosing to live your life by. If not, how can you match your behavior to your personal philosophy? This process will help you clarify the behavior that's most productive for you in pressing on. Use this approach whether the should is ladled out by you or someone else, either in person or over the Internet.

For example, you might ask yourself these two questions:

- Should I just work my job for the rest of my life, and be quiet and happy and satisfied with who I am now and what I've accomplished?
- Is this in keeping with my personal philosophy of life and the objectives I've set for myself, remembering I have only one life to live?

In order to determine the answers to these questions, refer to the five questions posed on page 31, addressing them one by one. Match your behavior to your personal philosophy.

Changing how you approach should creates new opportunities for growth. Hear what naysayers and *should*ers are saying—without guilt, think about it and make your choice in a firm, friendly, and fair way—then move on to do what you know is best for you.

5

Tame the Coulds, the Woulds, and the Shoulds

People love to give advice, often in areas where they aren't qualified. They think they know what you should do, and believe they can run your life better than you can. Those who indulge in this kind of behavior are often unhappy, jealous, embittered, stressed, or bored—hardly folks to emulate!

It's rare when should travels alone. Anyone who has *should*ed themselves, or has been *should*ed by others, knows this annoying command likes company.

Two of should's favorite traveling companions are would and could. But there's a specific reason should has paired up with those two—for cover.

While could might be used by someone who is truly respectful of you and wishes to give you options to consider, by and large, this isn't their intent. For most people, would and could are more than happy to provide should with every excuse it needs—it makes them appear reasonable.

Together, this trio operates like this: "I should have," "I could have," "I would have." Abbreviating it in "shorthand" then gives us: S/C/W—Should'a/Could'a/Would'a.

If you break it down, S/C/W looks like this…

Should **I Even Go There?**

Should is a command—whether it comes from you or someone else—typically used to gain control. While a *little* control may seem to be the intent of most *should*ers, what they're really after is absolute control. What starts as a casual interest in something or someone can quickly escalate into a complete takeover. The more control you give them, the more control they'll want.

Certain people love the feeling of power they get by lording should over others. For example, they may say things like: "You should clean up your act." "You should watch what you say." "You should show some respect." "You should give her a call." "You should send her a card." "You should wash the car!" Do you see how should controls if you follow through with the command? If you give in to should, you empower the *should*er and disempower yourself. Don't go there!

"I Could Do That, But..."—*It's Just an Excuse!*

This is often an excuse just waiting to be offered. While could can be used as an enabling word, it can also be used to introduce an excuse *not* to act. It provides a rational-sounding escape from responsible behavior, because could often travels with *but.*

"I could do that, but I don't have time," or "…I don't want to take advantage of my friends," or "…he probably wouldn't be interested." "Could, but…" often stands in the way of success. "I could do that, but my friends would laugh at me." "Why would I want to do that," our subconscious may ask, "when I really should keep doing what I'm doing, even though I hate it!"

People often inappropriately please others in an attempt to be liked, accepted, or out of fear of disturbing the status quo.

Consider Charles. He desperately wanted to leave his store manager job. In retail for 20 years, he figured if he built his own business, he could make more money, retire early, spend more time with his family, and generally be happier. They were good reasons for his optimism. Charles had seen friends from the retail profession go on to build businesses and earn great incomes.

"I should be right there with them," Charles thought. "Actually, I should really be ahead of them because, well, I'm always reading positive books and developing myself. I know what's going on. The freedom and potential of having your own business is a growing trend."

Charles thought about it a lot. He spent a lot of time *thinking* about building his own business and leaving his job, however, he couldn't get motivated enough to actually do it.

This is where a little innocent "but" reared its ugly head. "I could build my own business," Charles told himself, "*but* I might embarrass myself; my wife might not be interested; I wouldn't have enough time; I probably wouldn't be understood; and I sure wouldn't get discounted underwear at the store anymore!" This internal dialogue led to his decision not to take that first step toward business ownership that Charles was pretty sure he should!

Of course, the only thing that changed was that Charles got older and bitter, resenting the success of others. But he always wore new underwear! As for his dream…? Oh, well!

Is an "I could do that, but…" holding you back? Drop the but and say "I could do that, and I'm going to!"

The Three R's—*Responsibility, Realistic, and Rewards*

As mentioned before, could can be an enabling word. But all too often, many people run like crazy from the things that could empower them. Making a commitment implies *responsibility*, which a lot of people would rather avoid.

With responsibility comes the potential for finger-pointing and blame if things don't work out as they supposedly should. The report wasn't filed on time; the money-raising target wasn't reached;

the expected crowd didn't show; or the anticipated income level wasn't achieved—and *someone else* was responsible. So that *someone else* is to blame. But the problem is, and this is BIG!

When you blame, you give away your power!

We all have an amazing ability: In less than one second after a challenge is proposed or arises, each of us is perfectly capable of projecting the worst possible outcome. We may even convince ourselves that disaster is inevitable if we take on the challenge.

On the other hand, we are equally capable of projecting the best possible outcome for the same scenario. Sadly, however, instead of focusing on the prize, it's the *disaster* we too often see and buy into. We may have been led to believe we are incapable of producing or unworthy of achieving great results. Therefore, we never take the road that, with the right assistance and action, would have led us to success.

At the point of contemplating a change, there are basically two paths from which we can choose: continuing to follow the old familiar routine that is no longer giving us what we want, or pressing on toward a new objective that offers the possibility of a more positive, exciting, and fulfilling life.

For whatever reason, however, we often convince ourselves that the old, familiar routine is the one for us. We think we are being *realistic* so we never set big goals. That way, we're not too disappointed when a great outcome doesn't come our way. We don't understand that *realistic is simply whatever we believe*! We live our lives with diminished intentions. Quite predictably, the *lesser* objective delivers the *lesser* outcome—continuing to work in a job we dislike or one that doesn't pay very well.

The road of low intention simply isn't capable of giving you great rewards, so you never get the thrill of achieving them. What a sad, lackluster, uninspiring way to go.

Imagine what would happen if we all started pressing on toward a great objective of our own—the one that holds something more rewarding for us? This objective—when continuously pursued—would give us the greatest possible life experience. Where would we be then? More importantly, what opportunity might we have right now that, fully utilized, would allow us to create the life we aspire to live?

"I Would, But..."—*Is Yet Another Excuse*

Would is actually a different animal entirely from should and could. On its own, would implies that all those positive things that *might* be done probably won't be. And we tell ourselves that it's not for lack of effort. Well, actually, it *is* for lack of effort—the effort of taking the action we've been consciously or unconsciously avoiding.

Would is far too friendly with *but*, even more so than could. Would and *but* are an inseparable team in excuse-making.

"I would, but I'd just fall flat on my face," or "...my family will reject me," or "...I'd fail miserably," or "...I'm not talented." We stay right where we are, imagining the worst and never attempting anything new. To produce new outcomes, we need to get results by passionately taking *appropriate* action.

Of course, we're not alone in this. Others aren't beyond using would on us, just as we do on ourselves. They can do it just as easily as throwing should at us.

"You'd be a lot better off if you would just...." How many times have you heard this? It often comes from the same people who are masters of should. And, like should, it's used to exert control over you, often ending with "...do as I say—implied or otherwise."

In this case, would is should's softer version. It's intended to sound caring. But, in the end, they are only the feelings and concerns the advice givers have for themselves. Your wants and needs are a distant second—if considered at all.

That isn't to say you aren't important in this would scenario. You are *critical*. After all, advice givers need someone to give advice to. They have often let themselves down by not pressing on toward what they *truly* wanted. Therefore, they want to bring you down, too, so you don't get ahead and make them look bad. Misery loves company. But without your participation, advice givers can't play their game. Until a cooperative, unsuspecting acquiescing soul is found, there will be no one to manipulate. The *would*er will then be in the position of choosing whether or not to follow their *own* advice but, in most cases, they're too negative to do that. That's why they're giving advice. They want you in the box with them! They've taken their own dream-stealing advice and feel empty and frustrated. But that curbs neither their will to control nor their efforts to feel powerful and superior by attempting to thwart others in *their* efforts to succeed.

Advice Recipients Beware

People love to give advice, often in areas where they aren't qualified. They think they know what you should do, and they believe they can run your life better than you can. Those who indulge in this kind of behavior are often unhappy, jealous, embittered, stressed, or bored—hardly folks to emulate!

> *Some of them even use the Internet to blame others for their lack of success. Remember, naysayers are always good at making excuses, whether in person or over the Internet.*

Sometimes they'll tell you that their insight comes from personal trials and tribulations, even though they are hardly any wiser than you—they're just worn out from their hard-luck trip. Regardless of their ineptness at learning and growing to the point of reaching their "Someday I'll..." aspirations, they pretend to have great insight. They think they're able to look at *your* life objectively and fix it. And their saying "If I were you..." doesn't help you. In the end, it's a matter of control. Are you in control or are you giving control to the ever present advice givers who may show no evidence of having realized their own objectives?

Incessant advice givers appear to be intelligent and present a humane face to their so-called words of wisdom. At least, they tend to make suggestions that might seem reasonable—especially if someone is already looking for excuses not to do what he or she really wants to do. But their intent is the same as those who give should as a blatant command. They want to undermine your will and get you to do what *they* want you to do. They often feel threatened and fear your new interests or activities will cause you to outshine them, so they're afraid they'll lose you in the process. They try to get you off track and dampen your enterprising spirit. They believe that if they can't have what they want, why should anyone else—especially you?

*Should*ers who take a more "creative" (arrogant) tack usually approach a challenge (and you) with something along the lines of "*Humor* me." And here's the attitude of a condescending *shoul-d*er who's trying to weaken the other person and get his or her own way: "You should do what I want you to do. Since you're too dense to see my great wisdom and intellect, I'm going to have to slow way, *way* down so you can keep up. But because I like you (and you should respect me!), I'm going to indulge in this little game. Make no mistake about it, when we are done, I will have what I want—because I should." Shoulders may not say this in so many words, but their tone of voice and body language demonstrates an attitude of "I'm better than you."

This is just one alternative to coming out and *should*ing someone directly. The reason for using the just-humor-me disguise is that those on the receiving end of should tend to resent it. But even if they end up doing as they are told they should, sooner or later they dislike the situation, the task, the outcome and, very often, the person giving the advice. Why? Their dreams are nowhere to be found. No color, no clarity, nothing. They allowed someone else to should away their dreams.

> *The really crafty naysayers have found ways around the word should, but their agenda to get you to do what they want is still there.*

Is That *Really* a Question?

When does should, the statement, evolve into should, the question? It's a sly trick, typically practiced by only the most manipulative of people. Posed as a question, should frequently appears as: "Should you be doing that?" "Should you be saying that?" "Should you be eating that? "Should you"...whatever?

This really isn't much different than a direct should statement, but it has a less threatening, friendlier-sounding, concerned tone to it. Posing should as a question allows the speaker to say exactly what he or she wants, contrary to what *you* want—without appearing confrontational.

When it appears as a question, should allows you to reflect on how ridiculous the *should*er wants you to look and feel. It's just a way to coerce you through humiliation. Their efforts to shame are intended to weaken, so you'll be less certain of your own ideas and more receptive to theirs.

How About Shouldn't?

The question can take another, more undermining turn when it appears as shouldn't: "Shouldn't you just stop for a minute and think about the consequences?" "Shouldn't I be your first priority?" "Shouldn't the color really be purple, I mean, if you THINK about it?" "Shouldn't you just work your job and be satisfied with your life the way it is?"

Shouldn't is a whole lot more pointed, a whole lot nastier than should in its other forms. Rather than getting you to simply think, shouldn't can actually undermine you and the power you have to make your own decisions, but only if you allow it. It calls into question what you have in mind, or may have already begun carrying out, and labels it overtly or subtly as stupid or wrong.

Shouldn't says you had better reverse course now or suffer some horrible consequence. You've already botched things up, and your future efforts, from now on, will be totally devoted to cleaning up the impossible mess.

"Wouldn't" and "Won't"—*Both Members of the Same Family*

Wouldn't is a first cousin to shouldn't and can serve much the same purpose. But in a more overt way, it allows the questioner to say what he or she would personally *prefer* to see happen. Again, this is just the *opposite* of what you want, otherwise the person wouldn't have felt the need to use a condescending tone in an attempt to undermine your agenda.

At the same time, wouldn't tells you that the course you are on will lead to a disappointing or embarrassing outcome. This is apparent when you look at the two most infamous questions using this approach: "Wouldn't it make more sense to...?" and "Wouldn't you really rather...?"

Like a caterpillar, wouldn't can easily develop into its butterfly counterpart—*won't*. What makes won't so special is that it comes as a *warning*: "Won't that create more problems than it solves?" "Won't you lose money?" "Won't that make you fat?" "Won't everyone talk?" Won't deflates and negates even the best-laid plans—but only if we let it.

In all of these cases, the words tossed your way are simply meant to control your behavior. How you respond to them will make all the difference.

6

Beware of Those Who Speak in "Code"

The next time someone tells you what you should be doing and how you should be living your life, look what they've done and how they're living theirs.

For life's more calculating, often charming and disarming players, coming right out and actually saying the word should relays their agenda too bluntly. They know others will get their backs up and dig in their heels if they're told to do *anything*, much less that they *should* perform one way or another. They resort to more innocent sounding, covertly manipulative tactics.

Those who are too clever to say the word should rely on a grab bag of alternatives to impose their will on you and get you to do what they want. For anyone who thinks this way, there are many control mechanisms available to manipulate others.

Let's look at several examples of ways some people convey the idea, atmosphere, or attitude that should creates, without actually using the word. These statements are often manipulative, insinuating, and insulting, mostly coming in three forms: "I," "You," and "It."

First, the *"I"*s

In the world of things important, the "I" s have it. "I" this, "I" that, and "I" everything else. We tend to think of ourselves first, almost by default, and this makes it all too easy to lead with an "I." So when dispensing advice, most people draw first on their own experiences (and desires) when attempting to direct your behavior. They know where they've been, so it's easy to suggest that you go there too—even if it makes no sense at all. For example:

- ***I don't understand the problem.*** Said with a perplexed look, it is designed to have you think your concerns are really silly and, in the end, you should do what you are told. This implies that "I'm smarter than you and, because of that you should do as I say."
- ***I don't want to tell you what to do, but if you were smart about it you'd….*** This is just the beginning of a statement that is really a put down of the listener and ends with a strong suggestion telling you *exactly* what to do. While the speaker says he or she doesn't want to give you advice, that's precisely what that person is doing. Even though the word should isn't spoken, it's implied in so many *other* words, while the but negates the first phrase of the statement. Always beware of "but." It could be a put-down.
- ***I'm only watching out for your best interests.*** The speaker has first carefully considered how the situation will impact him or her. When he or she talks about looking out for you, this concern is really nothing more than an afterthought and is used to put you off guard. That person is decidedly first in his or her mind, and you are…well...second at best. That person wants you to do what's best for *him or her*—not you! They don't realize that, in the long run, what's best for you is really best for them too.

- ***I'd be afraid to try something like that.*** This means that "You're crazy and you shouldn't even think of doing it." But by presenting it in terms of him- or herself, the speaker really gets a two-for-one punch: control *and* an insult. They may even go so far as to tell you others have failed at it, implying you will too. What this really says is: "Pay attention to me because I know all the answers, and I don't want to see you fail." The speaker is implying that you are incapable of making appropriate choices for yourself.

- ***I could never wear that.*** The speaker has projected him- or herself onto the clothing you're wearing. This person is aghast to imagine what the reflection in the mirror would be with that particular color, design, or style—whatever he or she dislikes about your outfit.

  This also goes directly to taste, and tastes differ. You may look at yourself and see a prince or a princess, but the advice giver looks at the clothing and sees something else. You need to decide if you are going to a) subject yourself to this kind of abuse, b) change your wardrobe, or c) find another friend.

That takes care of the *"I"*s, or at least enough of them so you get the idea to be careful when someone starts trying to do your thinking for you.

Now, On to the *"You"*s

*"You"*s are different from *"I"s. "You"*s get right to the point. The speaker doesn't try to hide the fact that you are being told what to do. He or she desperately wants to manipulate you, but is going about it differently than using an *I* statement, to cushion the blow.

Your self-confidence is put to the test as well as your conviction about the direction you are going with your life. For example:

- ***You* can't *do this, that, or the other thing.*** This is the speaker's not-so-subtle inference that you are grossly incompetent. Rather than just being overbearing, "You can't" is an order essentially forbidding you to even make an effort in the direction of what you're considering. This goes *way* beyond "You shouldn't." It says you are incapable.

This might be appropriate for a six-year-old dragging a pogo stick toward the lip of the Grand Canyon, but it isn't appropriate for you—especially since we've already established that you are a mature adult. If you want to jump on the pogo stick near a very deep hole, it might not be the wisest move, but the choice, nonetheless, is entirely yours.

- ***You don't want that.*** The first thing to be aware of here, as in any should statement or its cousins, is the speaker's agenda. To help keep you open-minded and stir your thinking, however, here's an example of where this comment is actually true because the person does have your best interests at heart!

I overheard a conversation between a man and his wife at a grocery store checkout. She had reached for a copy of the *National Gossip Rag* and, silently, held it out to him. A little shake of the publication told him to put it into the cart. (It's wonderful how couples communicate without saying a word.)

Well, the *National Gossip Rag* is obviously nowhere on this man's radar screen. He stood there as if his wife were offering him a big sack of angry skunks. The idea of even *touching* the magazine was completely foreign and distasteful.

"You don't want that," he told her. What he was really saying is "You shouldn't be reading that garbage." Her response of more silent, determined shaking said, "Yes, I do." But after a few seconds, she said, "Maybe you have a point." Her response showed respect for his good judgment.

She stopped shaking the paper and the determined look on her face started to melt away. It was almost as if she realized she was just going back to old behaviors—mindless attractions and actions. It was beginning to occur to her that their money could be better spent on other more important things—things that could help them grow, rather than just be entertained. She shrugged her shoulders, put the *Rag* back on the stand, smiled, and they checked out.

Admittedly, this is an opposite example. It demonstrates, though, that the smart thing to say, in some cases, is "You're right, I don't want that." Yes, in some cases, the other person could be correct. In this instance, it appears as if this couple, especially the husband, has another agenda which no longer embraces reading as a frivolous escape, but rather as a tool for growth. In most cases, however, be wary of people who tell you, "You don't want that;" their agenda might not serve you.

- ***You've got a duty to….*** In the speaker's opinion, you *must* do what he or she thinks is important. It may not be of the least interest to you, but do it anyway!

  "You have a duty to take your Uncle Frank to the dog track. Now go!" This is a brazen, even more directive version of should, but it's a should nonetheless.

- ***You'd be much happier if you'd just….*** This is like a big ol' kindly should from Grandma or Grandpa. It comes from experience and disappointment. They are trying to save you from doing something they believed they were completely incapable of doing, or certainly incapable of doing *well.* They don't even want you to make an attempt at it. Doing things like going to college, taking a job out of town, starting your own business, or wanting to build your dream house are simply foreign to them.

  So, if you would just do as you're told—or not do any of the things you truly have your heart set on that he or she may have failed at—you'll be happy, like they are! (Then why don't they smile more often?)

- ***You'll never be in this position again.*** The rest of the statement reads, "…so you should take advantage of it now." This may well be true or it may not. But just because you're being pressured into doing something, doesn't mean it would be good for you to take advantage of it. Is doing something just because someone said you should the right course of action?

  Never allow yourself to be manipulated into doing anything, and don't try to manipulate another into doing anything either. Manipulation breeds resentment and hurts relationships. Instead, give people reasons why doing something would benefit them so they can make an informed decision.

- ***Are you really ready to do that?*** The message is essentially: "You're unfit, weak, dull, and unattractive. You're also a number of other negative things about which I won't go into detail now, but you know what they are." In summary, "You just can't do it!" This question only plants seeds of self-doubt.

  Rather than questioning one specific area that may be of actual concern, the questioner, often based on his or her own insecurities, is able to challenge your entire worth as a human being with one simple question. In the end, the message is, once again: "You should stay where you are. Settle for what you have. Don't aspire for more. And, for goodness sake, you should be happy with what you have."

  This raises an important question: Who is ever totally prepared for unexpected challenges and the increased responsibilities of greater success? It doesn't matter, you just keep going.

  Before he was launched into space atop a ten-story rocket for the first time, John Glenn had never done it before. Before he was sworn into office to take over for political legend FDR, Harry Truman hadn't served as President of the United States. Before Bill Gates developed Microsoft, he was nothing more than a *tinkerer* with a brilliant idea.

  But a more relevant question is: Are *you* really ready to move on with your life in a new and more productive way? Are you ready to leave the past behind where it belongs and start pressing on, going in your own direction with more vigor?

- ***Are you* sure *this is what you want?*** The message here is: "I heard what you said, but I think you're crazy! Furthermore, I would never do anything like that—and look how smart I am."

  Of course, you never hear this said directly, but this is what's implied. The person who's raising the question is essentially saying: "You're not in your right mind, so I'll do your thinking for you—and you should listen to me."

- ***Aren't you overreacting?*** Here, the speaker believes you can't be trusted with your thoughts and feelings. So he or she will nudge you in the right direction with the message: "You should just calm down and do what I say. Things will be fine."

- ***Things would go much more smoothly if you'd....*** Of course, this is just another toe-the-line statement, designed for you to do what the other person wants—it's a should. But this goes a step further. Here, there's an implied threat: "If you don't do as you're told, then you'll suffer the consequences."

  Consequences, in this case, can take as many forms as there are power balances in the world: employers/employees, parents/kids, leaders/followers, teachers/students, and large/small. Under these scenarios you can be fired, punished, failed, pounced upon, rejected, or dismissed.

- ***If it doesn't work out for you, just remember I told you so....*** Here the speaker assumes you'll fail even before you do anything! It's a putdown. The speaker is probably set in his or her ways. They're afraid to do new things so they try to hold you back as well. They may also not want you to outshine them and leave them behind.

  The statement, "If it doesn't work out...", plants the seed of a bad outcome even though you may be excited about moving on to something new. The speaker is suggesting that beyond the horizon, in the great unknown, lies disaster: "Gee, Christopher [Columbus], everyone knows the world is flat! When you sail off the edge, remember, I told you so."

- ***Think of someone other than yourself.*** The message the speaker really wants to convey but knows sounds a bit selfish is, "You should think of ME first."

  There's a saying that's been around for a long time that goes: "If you don't love yourself, it's impossible to truly love someone else." And it's true. If you don't care about yourself to do whatever it takes to give yourself the life you believe you deserve, how can you begin to be generous to others? You can't. Creating an environment in which you can grow and prosper in all areas of life also creates an atmosphere in which others can thrive, not just survive, as well.

- ***You just don't get it!*** This is where should takes a sharp turn toward inflicting injury. The speaker makes no effort to hide his or her contempt for your intelligence, believing he or she knows what's best. And if you can't see the brilliance of his or her plan or insight, he or she thinks you're stupid. You're a big disappointment and you should be excused to the kids' table at the next big family dinner.

  To add insult to injury, the speaker often goes one step further by also saying: "So let me explain it to you one more time." Attitudes like this are typically passed down from one generation to the next. Granddad spoke to Dad like this, and Dad had even less patience than Granddad, so look out when it comes your turn. The cross-generational message is this: "You don't have all the facts and you certainly aren't smart enough to handle them either, so you should rely on me to tell you how to think."

- ***Trust me!*** This typically conveys precisely the opposite of what the words actually mean. You are probably going to be taken advantage of and you should just get used it. If someone says *trust me*, then there is likely no basis for trust; and you would be wise *not to* trust. A truly trustworthy person doesn't need to say trust me. He or she simply exudes integrity. As the saying goes, "Who you are speaks so loudly, I cannot hear what you say."

Now, Let's Go On to the *"It"*s

It depersonalizes whatever is being said or whoever the speaker is attempting to criticize or control. The intended perception is that he or she is not trying to make you feel bad or manipulate you when that's exactly what that person is trying to do. Of course, this doesn't keep some people from throwing *I*s and *You*s into the mix, as you'll see. *It* is a lead-in to exerting control. For example:

- ***It wouldn't be fair to…the others, to me, or to you!*** This is a should angle with the agenda of bringing guilt and selfishness together in an ugly but powerful twosome—before you realize what's happening.

  This is a natural because so many people are willing to pass judgment on your behavior without knowing what's in your heart. If it's not what the speaker wants you to do and somehow your intended action is perceived as threatening, then it's automatically bad. This is especially true if it's what they wish they could do, but don't have the belief in themselves or the nerve to attempt it. If it's something the speaker had never personally thought of, and feels threatened because he or she doesn't understand, then it's immediately bad.

  The message is that you should just stay in your box and, of course, don't make a fuss about it. Then everyone will be happy—especially the speaker. But they'll be happy only until they brand you as an underachiever for not looking past the confines of your box.

- ***It's now or never!*** This is the fatalist's view of the world. He or she believes that if you don't act now you'll be lost. You'll be wandering in a personal desert for, oh, 40 years or more. So, you should act NOW!

  Maybe yes, maybe no. It's totally up to you. You may, however, do well by consulting with someone who is in life where you want to be.

  For example, buying a brand new car when you are just starting in your career or business, and need the money to invest in continuing education, isn't the best thing to do. So what if your neighbor bought one. He probably can't afford it either, but maybe he doesn't understand delayed gratification and the long-term detrimental effects of debt.

  Most people act on emotion, typically backed up with just enough information to make a decision. But, of course, some people won't act, even if they have all the information in the world. They aren't interested in changing their behaviors or outcomes; they are planted firmly in their comfort or familiar zones. They use their well-entrenched paralysis of analysis to keep them there—momentarily safe, but sorry in the long run. Some may tell you they would like to have a better life with greater rewards, but they're only entertaining or perhaps appeasing you—and kidding themselves.

As the adages go: "Actions speak louder than words"; "He who hesitates is lost"; and "Time waits for no one." And one thing is certainly true about "It's now or never": The sooner you do something, the sooner you can reach your objective.

- ***It's just the right thing to do.*** This can often be a legitimate statement, but it can also be used by someone who's trying to manipulate you into doing what they think you should do. Therefore, "It's just the right thing to do," can be subject to interpretation, depending on the credibility, honesty, and goodness of intention of the person saying it.

  For example, some believe that going to a big-name college is the right thing to do. And it may well be, for some. Others will tell you that going to work for a large corporation is the right thing to do. Still others will tell you that unless you can make your first million dollars by the time you're thirty, you had better go to work for someone else. They're essentially saying that tying your fate to someone else's dream is the right thing to do.

  The right thing to do is to search your soul and do what's best for you. Your friends, relatives, acquaintances, and others don't pay your bills or live your life. The essential question is this: "Whose objective are you pressing on toward?"

- ***Is it really worth it?*** This is another subtle attempt to undermine your efforts and dreams. It's usually said when the speaker believes and fears that you are about to overcome your obstacles and achieve your potential. This speaker may think you'll outgrow the relationship you have together, and outshine him or her. So, to avoid this possibility, he or she

> says, "Is it really worth it?" implying that you should just back off, and play it safe, accept life as it is.
>
> Now it's possible that what you are proposing to do, with enough dedication, may enable you to succeed beyond your wildest dreams. Then you'd have an answer to "Is it really worth it?" which would be a strong, positive "You bet!" The most successful people are keenly aware that hurdling life's obstacles is what molds us into the people we were created to be. It's one of life's greatest rewards.

We've just reviewed the undermining commands and suggestions others use in an attempt to manipulate our behavior—to get us to do what they want us to do—without using the word should. It may take some effort to understand those who speak in "code." But just pay attention and you can generally figure out what they really mean. In one example, just to keep you alert, we discussed a situation where you were told "You don't want that." In some cases this may be true, but what we want matters more to us than it does to anyone else. However, we're only likely to get it relative to the degree we take charge of our own lives and discontinue allowing others to control us.

So, what happens if you just do as you're told? You ignore yourself and stop pressing on? The damage this can do to your sense of well-being, and even your physical and mental health, can be immense.

The U.S. National Institute of Mental Health estimates that one in five adults—46 million people in the U.S. alone—suffer from a diagnosable mental disorder. How many of those cases of depression, anxiety, or panic are the result of chemical imbalances, we can only estimate. At the same time, *some* percentage of that staggeringly high number have had their life-changing challenges brought on by doing what *others* wanted them to do, ignoring what they knew was right *for themselves.*

Ideally, we'll take responsibility for what we do whenever we're given the opportunity. At the same time, after many years of habitually listening to others and following their directives to whatever degree, thinking and acting on your own behalf might not always be your initial response. You, like many others, may quickly acquiesce to others' desires because it may be the easiest thing to do at the time. Then again, you may be in the habit of delaying your response and find that considering advice from others may still be an important process—that is, if they care about you and are qualified to be advising you.

The next time others offer their wisdom, whether online or off, about how you should be living your life, apply this simple reality test: Look at their lives and how they're living them. Then ask yourself these ten questions:

- Are they doing what they truly desire?
- Are they fulfilled by what they're doing?
- Are they successful by your standards?
- Are they happy?
- Are they where you want to be?
- Are they a credible, trustworthy source of advice?
- How well do you know them?
- How well do they know you?
- Do they pay your bills?
- Do they care about you?

If the answer to each is *yes*, you may want to consider what the advice giver has to say. Otherwise, you may want to think twice about acting on unsolicited wisdom, especially the kind you might find over the Internet.

Wants, needs, goals, desires, and intentions are different for everyone. Other people's agendas about how we are to live are best subject to scrutiny. Put yourself and your family first when making those choices. Let go of the notion that should provides you with some kind of security blanket.

Use the free will you were born with, rather than automatically acquiescing to what others think you should or shouldn't do. You'll be much happier and more empowered to press on.

7

A Should by Any Other Name

When you truly care about others and compassionately focus on and address their wants and needs, they're more likely to follow you.

We're all affected by shades of should. Whether they come from us or someone else, the intended outcome of should and its gang of like-minded words is to get you to perform one way or another.

Two of the more widely used should substitutes—especially when it comes to work—are *have to* and *need to*. But there's a great deal of difference between them.

For starters, *have to* is a demand thought up by someone, or perhaps a nameless, faceless organization. It's a command to act. If whatever it is doesn't get done, it's implied that there will been dire consequences. Imagine yourself in a job situation where a deadline is looming. It almost implies that if you don't get this particular thing done, you or someone else will be in big trouble!

That was basically the situation I worked under for eleven years as a daily newspaper journalist—an investigative reporter. Having to meet deadlines was a way of life. Of course, it was important to meet timelines for a variety of reasons. Getting the paper out depended on it.

On any given day, most reporters in the newsroom are working on stories that will go to press in the paper's next edition. Their deadline is somewhere around 5 p.m. This was to ensure that a series of tightly orchestrated actions—editing, printing, and delivery the next morning—would take place. All of this has to happen in sequence. Each action is like a cog in a machine. Remove, jam, or break a cog and the machine shuts down. Without a deadline, there can be no paper.

In most other lines of work, deadlines come and go without the same level of pressure to meet them. Sure, it helps in planning workflows, especially when a large number of people are involved. However, in most cases, orders won't stop, and the staff will continue receiving money. But deadlines are imposed. They evoke a work ethic and control what gets done.

Like its cousin the deadline, *have to* is typically issued without much explanation. Those sending out the order don't feel compelled to give reasons why. *Have to* is enough of a reason as far as they're concerned, because, well, you should.

Have to is a lot more dictatorial than should; it doesn't even pretend to offer an explanation. You either do it or face serious consequences. *Have to* has a do-it-or-else implication. It leaves no room for doubt. Should can imply that there might be a choice. And in the newspaper business, as well as in many other job situations, *have to* is essential for successful operations. But outside of those arenas, *have to* could be used as a manipulation.

Have to is a stern approach that tends to make people's defenses go up before they have a chance to determine whether what they are told they *have to* do is even worthwhile. *Have to* doesn't encourage free enterprisers to cooperate and perform, even though it's useful when referring to rules, regulations, laws, and ethics. For example, business owners have escaped a bureaucratic structure or are in the process of doing so, and they certainly don't want to hear the words *have to* from a mentor or leader. If they do they may retort, "I don't need another job," or "I got enough of that when I had a boss."

In free enterprise organizations where everyone has his or her own business, leaders don't have the formal power to come right out and tell their associates they *have to* do anything. In reality, nobody has to do anything. In fact, they can choose to do nothing—and fail! But when it comes to a team effort, each team member *needs to* do certain things in order to achieve success. Everyone *needs to* do his or her part to be a viable member of the team and achieve goals.

"Need to" Can Aid in Team Building

Need to is more caring than should, and sends a different message than *have to*. Even though it can be somewhat associated with should, *need to* suggests that you do something to achieve the particular result you desire. For example, *if* you want to go to the next level in your business or career, you *need to* do certain things. Here it would be appropriate for a leader or mentor to inform you of what you *need to* do to get a particular result.

If what you're doing requires the cooperative teamwork of like-minded people, as most things in life do, *need to* can be used within the context that everyone associated contributes not only for their own growth, but for the growth of others as well. Everyone doing what he or she *needs to* do helps create a larger win/win situation that benefits all concerned. Nothing of much significance can be accomplished alone. When used in the context of accomplishing a goal, *need to* establishes a sense of urgency and excitement.

Leaders who say you *need to* are more inclined either to mentor you themselves or refer you to someone else who will, provided you're humble enough to follow their direction. They'll encourage and, perhaps, even assist those who are committed to taking action. Everyone's participation is welcomed, but no one particular person's participation is essential. If someone doesn't want to be a team player, that's okay. The leader will simply search for and work with someone else who does. If someone is not willing to listen to the leader's *need to* suggestions and follow whatever system may be in place, then that person's association with the organization won't work.

> *Using* need to *encourages a cooperative effort and often leads to greater understanding and stronger team building.*

Always aim for a win/win situation to create an atmosphere of harmony, trust, respect, and friendship where people want to stay. It sets the stage for a synergistic atmosphere where together everyone participating accomplishes more for his or her efforts than if he or she were to work along. It also serves to attract more people to join the team.

If People Observe Bad Behavior on Your Part, *Don't Expect Them to Follow Your Good Advice*

Perceptions are important. Even when they might be wrong or a little distorted, what people think and how they are affected emotionally dictates how they'll react or respond. Here, responding is more thoughtful and less likely to be automatically negative. If you operate inside the box of should, you'll send negative signals to your team members. The fallout for you will be real and unkind whether it's immediately obvious or not.

First, everyone around the situation will know whether you're a *have to* or a *need to* person—or simply a *should*er—and they'll act accordingly. Some will ignore you. Some will run. Others will lay traps and wait for you to fall into them. How the team members choose to react or respond is something every *should*er would be wise to consider. But unfortunately most don't bother. Instead, they throw shoulds around without realizing how they negatively affect the quality of their relationships.

Being fair, considerate, flexible, and willing to compromise is to everyone's advantage. You convey who you are and how much you care by your interactions with others, attitude toward them, work ethic and the words, in general, that come out of your mouth. The list goes on and on. "Leading by example" comes out of this environment. If you are a leader or aspiring to be one, others are more likely to follow and duplicate you when you do the right and kind thing.

Second, if the *should*er is doing his or her *should*ing in a work relationship, it will only deteriorate as time goes on. Productivity diminishes without obvious reasons, calls aren't returned, and sarcastic remarks increase.

Of course, *one* bad encounter doesn't mean every other encounter will be awful. But two, three, or more bad experiences indicate a trend. This establishes a pattern and, once again, the *should*er can expect some fallout. And only when the pattern changes for the good (to win/win), can the future be bright.

Third, the *should*er has to live with him- or herself. It's a lot easier to look at yourself in the mirror each morning when you haven't spent the previous day terrorizing people with should or its cousins.

If you're constantly making demands or trying to bully others into actions they don't want to take, you'll have trouble building positive relationships, and thus, your career or business. People form opinions and take action based on what they observe. When it's brutish behavior they see or experience, *should*ees' responses often take the form of retaliation. If people observe bad behavior on your part, don't expect them to follow your good advice. They're more likely to do what you do rather than what you say.

When you truly care about others and compassionately focus on and address their wants and needs, they're more likely to follow you. They see that you have no hidden agenda. Common goals can be identified and worked toward. Learning to cooperate and look out for each other becomes the norm. Should, *have to*, and all the rest of those manipulative directives become a thing of the past.

8

Beware of Tyrants' Tactics

Naysayers, like an overbearing boss, typically don't want a lot of dialogue. It would only hold out the possibility of another opinion, or another way of doing things.

It seems as though we all fit into some kind of category. And if we don't readily line up under a neat, narrow heading, others are more than happy to create a category *for* us.

While you may not instantly think of categories of people, and do your best to treat everyone as an individual, it is helpful to group them when you're working to gain a better understanding of should. There are some very distinct similarities and differences in approaches and attitudes as people try to should others into action.

Here we'll take a look at the extreme cases, as well as the more benign ones. These *should*ers offer a hand, but then explain in their own soft, or not so soft, calculated words just exactly the way things should go. But no one wants to follow a people like that. They are tyrants operating under the old intimidation model, rather than fine leaders who influence others with integrity and by good example.

Two Ends of the Should-Style Spectrum—*Soft* Should*ers* *and Whip Crackers*

To protect yourself from being negatively influenced by *should*ers and not be one yourself, you need to become more aware of the tactics employed by particular categories of *shoulders*. Of course, we all know the *soft should*ers. Their daily ritual often includes sweetly saying things like "Yes, dear, you really should…" Their tone of voice is so endearing and innocent sounding that it takes you off guard.

At the overt end of the spectrum are the *whip crackers*. These people, regardless of gender, love to give orders, and shoulds are their primary method for delivering them. You've no doubt seen them. You may even work for one! Or, heaven forbid, you might even be one! But just in case you've *never* had the pleasure, whip crackers behave something like this:

> It's 8 a.m. on a Monday. You're at your desk going over your sales figures for the previous week. Out of the corner of your eye, you see the boss drawing near. You look up from your desk and cheerfully say "Good morning!"
>
> The whip cracker then responds in one of three ways by saying:
>
> - ***"Well?"*** With this response, the boss expects you to immediately start reciting your numbers. The response "good morning" doesn't seem to be in his or her vocabulary.
> - ***"In my office!"*** Here, the boss not only wants your numbers, but also a full rundown of what your sales projections are for next month. Furthermore, he or she also wants a detailed outline of all the new territories you'll be opening up *next* year—even if it's still the beginning of *this* year!
> - ***"I wouldn't bet on it."*** This response relays the height of exerting control. Not only does it ignore your efforts to be pleasantly civil, but it can also be used to invoke an element of fear.

In each case, the message of "You should be doing more than you are" is inescapable. Whip crackers are notorious for this. While they may be the most difficult to work with, the ironic thing is that whip crackers are typically the *easiest* to deal with. But without some major creativity, you simply can't negotiate with them, win their empathy, or be their friend; not even close. However, you'll know exactly where you stand, and can start putting together a response plan.

There is no ambiguity about whip crackers. They operate in the sharp, contrasting worlds of black or white, do or don't, live or die, please me or you'll lose your job.

In Between Soft *Should*ers and Whip Crackers

Of course, not everyone who uses should is a soft *should*er or whip cracker. There are plenty of other in-between types who are more than happy to tell you what you should be thinking or doing, and how you should be living your life! They might even tell you that your dreams and goals are silly or unrealistic. But remember, realistic is simply whatever you *believe*. It doesn't matter what they believe when it's your dream or goal at stake. They're just trying to impose a limitation on you or others for whatever reason.

Most *should*ers are not as subtle as soft *should*ers or as direct as whip crackers; they just use different approaches. In the end though, they want the same thing—to control you to whatever degree. They just go about it in different ways, depending on their personalities and what they believe is the best tactic.

When dealing with a *should*er who is less than direct, be aware of his or her manipulative tactics. Some resourcefulness will help you gain clarity of the speaker's agenda, and your commitment to your priorities will give you the edge. Your growing understanding of the world of should will help you control any tendency you may have to just automatically do what someone else wants, whether it's in your best interest or not.

You'll be strong enough not to yield to manipulation just to escape any discomfort you may feel at the moment.

*Should*ers use a vast array of approaches to convey messages that you should be doing things differently. They often try to keep you in the status quo by trying to manipulate you into changing your behavior. Here are some examples:

- ***Charmers***—These folks often have big egos. They're great at "dressing things up" on the agenda that they want others to follow, presenting them in an impressive way. But after everyone has been duly convinced to participate, the real agenda starts to emerge. Charmers are great at smoke-screening. They use a lot of ingredients and waste a lot of time concocting something that looks good on the outside but is virtually worthless at its core. "You should be clever like me" is the message charmers are only too happy to convey.

- ***Reactors***—These people are good at standing idly by while others go off and mess things up. They're too lazy to help out, and they contribute only after the fact. They come across as though they know all the answers. Their so-called cleanup is often accompanied by a lot of muttering, head shaking, huffing and puffing, sighing, and staring into space. "You idiots should have done it my way" is their message. They get pleasure out of being critical, yet conveniently refuse to help others do things right from the get go.

- ***Hammers***—This is the category of simple, direct brutes, pounding on others to get them into shape or beat them into submission. They repeatedly hold others to the fire and then pull them out—like a blacksmith—only to put them on an anvil and hit them with a hammer. Sooner or later, they pound others into the shape they want. The recipient of this sort of assault is usually rendered intimidated and virtually lifeless. But the person with should in mind, regardless of the unkindness of the method, has gotten the recipient into the exact shape he or she was after.

An overbearing boss is a good example of the mindset of such a *should*er. They typically do not want any dialogue because it holds out the possibility of another opinion or another way of doing something. They don't want people to think—knowing that an insight about an alternative way might cause resistance. Hammers and whip crackers are closely related.

- ***Conivers***—These folks are the opposite of hammers. They are accustomed to stealthily maneuvering others with an apparently soft, warm touch into the place where they should be—a place from which it is nearly impossible to extract themselves. They often convince others for a lot of the wrong reasons. The conniver's manipulation involves deluding you with his or her ideas and attention lest you stray from the intended agenda.

- ***Preservers***—Quietly and systematically, these folks try to keep others in boxes—environments in which the preserver wants them to stay. They bury the boxed people so deep that they may never be heard from again. Softly spoken "Shhhs" and "Ohhhs" are among their supposedly comforting tones that translate directly to should. Their message is often to play it safe. For example, whenever you share your dream or objective and how you plan to go about achieving it, they might say something like, "Ohhh, you're going to do *that*?" Or they could say, "Shhh, don't let your father hear you say you're going to do *that*. He always wanted you to be a...."

- ***Freeloaders***—These folks are master manipulators. But those who are onto their game of eliciting pity and undeserved support handle these burdensome beings appropriately—quickly and efficiently. Time is on the freeloaders' side though. They can wait if there is a bit of a delay in help arriving. Freeloaders have all the time in the world, because they do virtually nothing. Entitlement is their mindset, and they'll go from one unsuspecting soul to the next in their efforts to be taken care of as they believe they should. Those who have let themselves fall into a freeloader's trap and be used and abused, have one goal in mind: dispatching the freeloader as quickly as possible to avoid being taken advantage of anymore. Letting go of the freeloader results in a tremendous feeling of liberation.

- ***Users***—Users step on others to achieve their goals, with no regard for them or their feelings. Should is implied, since they typically don't say much. They're rude and crude and have an attitude that says, in essence, "You should do what I say or get out of my way. I'm aggressive and, if you don't move, I'll simply trample you to get where I'm going." Whip cracking happens in the user's head rather than overtly. At first they may come across as winners, but after you get to know them, you won't want to associate with them.

- ***Fixers***—These people are dangerous because they enter the environment to a chorus of high praise and even greater expectations. When they align themselves with a corporation, for example, they are usually answerable to only one person, so they are given quite a bit of power. They typically issue a report that recommends how everyone—including you—should behave, even though they have never heard of you or your company until they were invited to submit a bid. Fixers put on an air of authority that leads others to believe they have all the answers, when, in fact, they don't.

This is just a sampling of the approaches some people use in an attempt to get you to behave as they believe you should. But remember, the only power they really have is that which you give them. So, whether you surrender to another's will or not is your choice. Standing up to them requires you to do precisely that: *Stand up to them.* Stiffen your spine and your resolve and do what you believe you need to do for yourself and your family.

9

Sometimes Should Is Good

Another situation where should is good occurs when you are fortunate enough to have a leader or mentor who cares about you enough to help.

There are exceptions to not using should—special circumstances where it is actually good to use should.

First, there are parents to consider. Until we reach age 18 (and sometimes beyond!), parents often suggest various ways we should behave. And especially when dealing with a very young or immature child, this is the way it needs to be. For example, who would ever allow themselves to be potty trained, when the alternative—going whenever and wherever he or she likes—is so much easier?

Once you get the basics out of the way, and parents feel that their imprint has been pretty well made on you, the nature of should changes. And it typically comes around less and less frequently. When it does, however, it is generally meant to convey wisdom rather than to control. This is so when parents nurture their children to become fully functioning, independent-thinking human beings, and treat them as such.

Another exception to the world of should are drill sergeants and anyone in the military whose rank is higher than yours. Here it's necessary to create and maintain order and uniformity of behavior, especially when chaos is breaking out all around.

The military command, "That's an order!" which is an absolute should, is meant for the greater good. Most civilians would say, "Hey, let's talk about it!" or "I have another idea." But it's quite clear that the armed forces cannot be debating societies.

Another situation where should can be good for you occurs when you are fortunate enough to have a leader or mentor who cares about you enough to help. This is rare, indeed, and something to be treasured. These people tell you what to do and set the example of how to do it *so you can be successful like they are.* Paying careful attention to these voices of experience is essential for you to achieve the results you want.

Yes, there are special circumstances when should is necessary and appropriate.

Ultimately, however, you are always responsible for yourself and the outcomes you create, regardless of what anyone says you should or shouldn't do, or how they go about saying it.

10

Just Do What You're Told

Shoulds take you off track and don't play a role in the outcomes you really want. Shoulds are mainly about the agendas of others.

If you're looking for the easiest way through life, here it is: Simply agree to seven magic words and you'll never have to lift another mental finger as long as you live. You'll never have to tolerate a different thought, create a better solution, or produce a unique outcome—ever again. So what are those magic words? *This is the way it should be.*

Of course, acting on those seven words has its advantages. It doesn't require a second of new thinking and it totally shuns creativity. Not only is the person giving the should order saved from exercising his or her brain, so is anyone who quietly carries it out. Suddenly, life seems to be easier, but it doesn't stay that way for long.

Some things interfere with feeling comfortable about using this approach to life, for example: guilt for not standing up for yourself; greater aspirations; value differences; and uncertainty about whether the person *should*ing truly has your best interests at heart. Beyond these calls to conscience, two key questions hover in the background: "Is this what I really want?" and "What about my dream?"

Do you want to be like many others who blindly give in to those issuing should orders from *The Status Quo Handbook of Life*? Should takes you off track and don't play a role in the outcomes *you* really want. Shoulds are mainly about the agendas of others.

The world demands that people think and do like the masses who generally don't get very far in life. Always submitting to other people's wishes when they're not in our best interest thwarts positive growth, working effectively, producing maximally, happiness, success, and making a difference. Should has virtually no place in our lives if we want to move ahead. It keeps us marching to someone else's beat—not our own.

At the same time, as we learn and grow, doing new things makes certain demands:

- First, it demands that industries, governments, and societies question their direction and take responsibility for their actions.

- Second, it requires that people actually analyze situations before they begin to take action to deal with them.

- Third, it asks that people listen to others with a more intelligent, empathetic ear rather than with a fixed, controlling agenda.

Thinking about issues, situations, and people in different and more productive ways requires a little more focus, a bit more work. But what you'll get out of the process will provide you with a range of solutions with which you can successfully ride long into the future.

Thomas Edison and *Old Thinking*

Consider Thomas Edison and one of his greatest inventions—the "talking machine"—the phonograph. He stumbled onto this new technology while working on telephones and telegraphs, looking for a way to automatically record phone messages. It wasn't something he intended to invent to entertain people. He thought of it more as voice mail.

But that was Edison and that was *then*, you may be thinking. In a world where virtually everything new is done for us and rolled out in the three months before the holidays, why bother to think in new ways and devise new things?

How many people want to put themselves out or risk failure by doing something new? How many people think like entrepreneurs, have a sense of adventure, and do something to make a difference? How many people live on the edge of wonderful new beginnings every day as they happily press on toward the life they want?

Most people certainly don't think like Edison, who invented great new things by working to improve on the great things he'd already invented. Who wants to be bothered taking a risk? After all, there's a bottom line for everything. As often happens in the workplace, innovative ideas that require what may be perceived as too much of an investment are doomed.

Here's the so-called logic from status quo people who issue "It shouldn't be done" directives in the traditional corporate work environment: "We already manufacture a completely adequate product for that particular situation. So, why would you want to go to the expense of creating a so-called better product when one, especially one that's just *fine*, already exists? Just be satisfied with the product we have in inventory, then move on to what you were doing."

A Healthy, Open Attitude Toward Accepting Change

In 1907, there was a challenge. Phone conversations couldn't be carried out over long distances. Something was needed to amplify the voices if they were to be carried from one city to the next. This spawned the birth of the vacuum tube.

But, of course, vacuum tubes didn't last very long. They couldn't. They failed regularly and consumed too much power, while producing too much heat. As a result, four decades later, the solid-state semiconductor was invented to replace the once awe-inspiring tube. The semiconductor evolved into the transistor and, finally, the integrated circuit. The latter has been responsible for smaller computers, space flight, safer automobiles, and nearly every appliance we use. So much for anyone who denies the value of those early efforts to transmit voices over a wire.

If technology doesn't present enough of a case, look at the differences in attitudes between your parents' time and now. The perspective on limits has changed. This certainly isn't to say that the baseline for good and reasonable behavior has been moved. It's just that people are more willing to challenge established ways of doing things that have proven to be ineffective. Accepting should and always being a robotic must-do, is now, more than ever, not the only option.

Whether this has created situations that are better or worse is for you to decide. But the questioners' willingness to challenge the status quo, to voice a healthy skepticism of the way things have always been done has changed the way we look at the world. This attitude has helped to create an evolving world more open to different solutions and new opportunities.

From Impossibilities to—*Dreams Do Come True*

Today, with the ease of communicating worldwide and sharing information, change can happen faster than ever. Operating methods can become old overnight and stresses have increased, especially in the everyday working world. In many cases, staffing has decreased, causing overloads on employees endeavoring to keep the corporate boat afloat. We're bombarded with ideas; competition isn't just with the company across town, but with everyone on Earth.

The focus today, especially for upstanding business owners and career-oriented people, is to make a difference—leave a legacy. Those who care about others as they build their businesses or careers can accomplish that. They win in the long run.

Technology, as convenient as it makes communications, cannot replace old-fashioned kindness. New perspectives represent change. And this can be good as long as the change agents are doing their best to do the right thing for everyone concerned. Accepting should from someone who was schooled in hard, so-called unbreakable rules—that no longer apply—isn't the ticket to realizing our potential for doing more good and being appropriately rewarded.

Average-thinking people believe that just because something has been done a certain way for decades, there's no room for improvement. It's wise to do things differently if a challenge is called for, for example, as technology improves. It'll make a difference in the quality of your life. Just look at what the Internet has done for the world.

How often are changes needed? How often do all the factors at play in any relationship, agreement, or business interaction remain the same? What happens when only one person or element in the mix begins to grow or evolve? The other person or element needs to grow or evolve to rebalance the situation. What happens when the need for change overcomes the status quo of should? You go from vacuum tubes and transistors to wireless—from impossibilities to *dreams do come true.*

11

It's Time to Get Out of Any "Boxes" You May Be In

Once we wake up and identify any boxes we may be in, they're impossible to ignore. This can ignite the spark that helps us break through any limitations we thought we had. We can then discover who we really are and what we can accomplish when we take action.

Responding to *should*ers' ideas, directions, and shoulds puts you in a box—the one-way, dream-stifling box of the average-thinking person. A lot has been written about the box: living inside the box, escaping the box, thinking outside the box. The list goes on and on.

The box discussion, whatever form it takes, doesn't end—it's pervasive. It's not going away, regardless of how much discussion takes place about it, despite the fact that people may want to dismiss it as last year's topic. The box persists in people's lives because many people *like* the box. Ask them and they'll deny it. They're apt to say, "No, not me. I hate the box. And if anyone tries to force me into one, they'll be in trouble."

But if you don't call a situation a box, it's much easier to handle. People relate to box-type environments the same way most pets respond to cages.

Now you may look at a little dog in a cage and say, "Oh, you poor thing, cooped up inside like that. You must be miserable." You shake your head and pity the poor little dog.

But the dog looks back and thinks, "No way you're taking me out of here, and there is definitely no way you are getting *inside* of my box! There is only room for one of us inside this safe, warm place where I don't have to worry about anyone else hurting me. Now, *go away*. Woof!"

A Safe But Sorry Place to Call My Own

Put someone in a safe, warm environment, where most of his (or her) needs are met and some wishes are granted, and he's likely to grab it in a second. Call the environment a box, though, and he'll have no part of it. At least, that's probably what he'll tell you. But in three out of four cases, once the pressure is off, and outsiders are no longer looking, he'll call the owner of the box and ask what arrangements can be made to get inside of it.

Again, it is never called a box but, instead, a situation or position. Boxes go by names like corporation, firm, department, agency, city, division, and state. Many offer good benefits, a retirement plan, and some measure of predictability—until someone boots you out. Regardless, many people want in—desperately. Sad to say, it's the way the majority of people think life should be.

People allow themselves to be trapped in boxes, especially when routine replaces challenges, complacency drives away necessary innovation, and potential is thwarted rather than nurtured. Sadly, they are their own worst enemies.

Boxes come in many shapes, sizes, and concepts. That's why they can creep virtually unnoticed into our lives and present themselves as inevitable facts of life. But once we wake up and identify any boxes we may be in, they're impossible to ignore.

This can ignite the spark that helps us break through any limitations we thought we had. We can then discover who we really are and what we can accomplish when we take action.

Should is stealthy. It will seize nearly any opportunity to slip into your life and try to force you into various boxes—situations, obligations, and other entrapments you may initially agree to but later regret. Unfortunately, most of these cases play out because of manipulative, convincing people who have an agenda different than yours.

Those who try to get you into these behavioral boxes and try to put the lid on it if you threaten to rise up out of them, can be quite resourceful. So knowing when should is likely to occur and the form it may take will help you anticipate it, respond to it, and effectively deal with it.

Sounds a Bit Forced

Some *should*ers are analytical, linear, and dogmatic in dispensing shoulds. They not only assess how to deal with the problem, your life and your behaviors, but endlessly analyze why this situation even exists. These people are motivated by finding the root cause, the elements that sustain it, the areas where it can spread, and a dozen other extrapolations surrounding the so-called problem.

Their solution can be executed only by taking specific, logical, and orderly steps to get you to go along with their agenda. If the solution-finding campaign stalls, it must be dealt with before anything else can be done to address other facets of the situation. Listening to this kind of advice can freeze you in a rut-perpetuating place virtually forever. "The solution," they announce, after a staggeringly long investigation—paralysis of analysis—is "a should be...." Among their more practiced lines is, "It only makes sense." So, beware!

Another type of *should*er relies exclusively on rules, precedent, charters, founding documents, and other paperwork in efforts to guide your behavior. Precedent is high on this group's list of approaches that *should* be used, especially when they are looking for some sort of victory that may or may not benefit you.

In most cases, these people are very accommodating. They want you to believe you have gotten your way even in the face of defeat. The next step is for them to advise you—in no uncertain terms—how you should respond to your new situation. When dealing with these folks, beware of the assurance "I'm doing this for you!"

Grounds for Advice

Other *shoulder*s are more grounded in creatively dispensing their advice. As a rule, they believe the way the world should work is based on what sounds good to them. Be extremely careful how you even approach these people, let alone how you measure their advice.

For them, the illogical makes for interesting life twists and turns. If they can get you to buy a novel approach, they believe they've done something good. How you deal with the consequences, well, that's up to you. You know you're dealing with a creative *shoulder* when you hear the words "Doesn't that sound like fun?"

Abstract thinkers are another group that excels in telling you what they believe you should hear. Their concept of should depends solely on what's important to them—*not you!*

Here, pay special attention to who's giving the advice. If it's important for you to gain self-knowledge, beware of someone who suggests you should be focusing on absolute truth and then goes on to define it in a way that suggests you stay in your box. Metaphors play a big role in the world these people inhabit. One is just as likely to tell you how to reach the top of the mountain when you're seeking marital advice. Among the lines favored by this group is, "Think about it!"

Finally, there are those whose tendency is to comfort, protect, and hover. Should comes from them sounding very much like "You should eat." This quickly evolves into "You should eat more!" This is inevitably followed by the instructions: You should find a girlfriend, a nice boy, and, predictably, a job.

Laced throughout all of this *should*er's priorities are varying degrees of guilt-inducing statements selected to keep you in line and afraid to do anything potentially disagreeable to the *should*er. The intentions may seem good, but the result is stifling in most cases. Such people are often rigid and paranoid about saying you should follow the crowd, and they try to push others into following certain rules. This is the one element that's unique to this class of advice-givers.

The challenge is that all of these people, regardless of the roles they play, seem to ignore the fact that it's your life and your prerogative on how to live it. Just because they let shoulds stop them, you don't need to let shoulds stop you! Most of them are living a life of regret, and they fear leaving their boring little boxes where they are complacently passing the time. Those who tell you that living your life should be done this way or that, simply don't see the world the way you do. They are focused on problems rather than possibilities. More often than not, they want you to buy into their world and abandon yours.

Advice can certainly be helpful, and even essential, if it's positive and productive, and makes sense with what you are endeavoring to do. But is that person where you want to be or on the way to it? Does he or she care about *your* objectives? Is the advice objective-thwarting or objective-supporting? As long as it's win/win, advice can often be a source of comfort, direction, encouragement, and assurance.

Gauge the merit of advice, and keep an eye on how it could impact you. Be especially cautious when you suspect it may tempt you to stay in a box you want to get out of or even lead you toward another box you don't want to be in!

12

Whose Roadmap, Recipe, or Agenda Are You Following?

Agreeing with naysayers is a dangerous trap. Even without bars across the windows, or walls of concrete to keep you inside, you live your life in custody.

There's a fine line between proceeding with your life in the direction you choose and just putting up with the challenges you face daily because you've been told you should.

Ironically, there's one thing most people won't admit to in ignoring what they want and playing along with should: Going with should allows them to be *lazy*. But laziness is an obstacle to be overcome for people who are serious about pressing on.

If inappropriate shoulds are in the driver's seat, you aren't doing what's important to move forward—whatever creative, outrageous, or innovative task would be your next step in making your life more of what you want it to be. You're no longer actively invested in your life. The person you *can* be has taken a backseat. He or she is reading novels rather than personal growth books—escaping reality rather than changing it, or has gladly been placed in confinement. The person directing your life is anyone…but not you.

We talked earlier about living life trapped in a box. Going along with naysayers is a dangerous trap. Even without bars across the windows, or walls of concrete to keep you inside, you live your life in custody.

Reporting to where you've been assigned at the prescribed hour, eating each meal from a menu of one item, and following the same unrewarding course you may have for years, represent the ultimate surrender to should. You might as well be trapped in a box.

Searching for Alternatives

If you live your life without thinking—without being conscious of your choices—you're only fulfilling *other* people's desires. Life is no more complex than following their clearly defined path. The problem is that while the daily grind may be simple, it leads many to ask, "What's the point?"

"Just do as you're told and you'll be fine," the boss says. If what you want is *exactly* what he or she wants, life is great. But how often is the boss focused on helping you get what *you* want? How often do working people have a true support network? If you have or find one, treasure it and take full advantage of the opportunity it offers.

What if you don't have all the ingredients or the desire to continue doing what the boss says, while forsaking your own desires? What can you do? Improvise? I don't think so. Improvisation and should don't live in the same neighborhood. Personal aims aren't even within earshot.

You may love your job and think this is all pretty far-fetched. But what if you don't love your job or some aspect of it? Don't you want to find an alternative road? What's preventing you from pressing on until you get what you want? Since there's no convenient time, what are you waiting for?

If only this were the case. If goal-oriented people were only more numerous, the world would be a better place. There would be less resentment and anger. There would be less road rage and fewer frustrated people. More people would be living the life they want, or at least pressing on toward it. Self-reliance, purpose, and responsibility would be the norm, and the words "I can't" or "that's impossible" would be laughable things of the past. If everyone would think in terms of empowering him- or herself and taking personal responsibility—while supporting others in doing the same—more of us would be motivated to chart our own course.

In the short-run, it seems as though should makes things easier to deal with, whether it's at work, with your family, or in social relationships. It may seem easier to please people, get their approval, and not rock the boat. It may seem that when you don't have to think, analyze, or prioritize, some of life's challenges disappear. But life's finest rewards vanish right along with them. Unconsciously yielding to shoulds, day in and day out, leads to long-term pain and regret. Clearly, this is not the recommended choice for anyone seeking a better life.

A Choice of One

Another problem arises when sticking to a plan that leads only to the fruition of someone else's agenda. You may not really want to go where their road leads. Instead, you may want to do something else that is different than what that agenda calls for.

Consider this: You have a recipe for apple pie. But today, you decide you're not really in the mood for apple; you want cherry. So you're left with a choice: Do you deviate from the cookbook's stay-within-the-lines recipe, or just do as you're told—what you should do as called for in the recipe?

If you're acting according to should, it's apple pie you'll get—want it or not. You'd better be happy about it and not complain. The directions don't care about cherries, so why should you? Anyway, if you were an average, stay-in-the-box, should-abiding citizen, you wouldn't give a whit about cherries, so why wouldn't you put them out of your mind? There, isn't that better? You don't even have to think about cherries. Apples are good enough. After all, apples are what the recipe calls for. You like apples, anyway, right? There, that wasn't so bad now, was it? After all, you're used to accepting what you don't want, aren't you?

Just think, with should, you can coast along—maybe forever—and not have to fret over an independent thought (let alone an exciting one!) ever again. Should allows just one way of thinking, acting, and doing things, regardless of whether it supports you in your quest. The thought of cherry pie never enters your mind again. But neither does ice cream, cake, or chocolate. Those in the should camp may tell you that too many choices only complicate things. They may, with warning fingers pointed at you, say you should play it safe. But exactly where has that thinking carried *them*? Most likely not where they want to be.

Acting according to should keeps you walking the straight and narrow—on someone else's road to success. You use the same group of muscles and brain synapses over and over again. You just don't have to think. But sadly, you don't get to dance, dream, experiment, stretch, or grow either. You don't get the stimulation that comes only from being on the quest for a better tomorrow.

Keep the Should—*Give Me Teflon!*

What happens when you start thinking in terms of alternatives to the ruts of should?

Consider one event in the 1930s in the duPont labs. In an effort to create a new cooling agent to replace the expensive refrigerant Freon, scientist Roy Plunkett decided to run an experiment by combining tetrafluoroethylene (TFE) and hydrochloric acid. On its face, the result appeared to be a wasteful and time-consuming failure. It certainly wasn't what Plunkett was looking for when he started out.

At that point, Plunkett realized he didn't get the result he thought he should have, and it would've been easy to ignore it or write it off as a misguided fiasco. But the substance turned out to be the never-before-seen polymer we now call Teflon.

If Plunkett and his team had been operating according to should, Teflon may not have been invented, or at least its development would have been delayed until someone else had the chutzpa to ignore should. Hundreds of industrial uses—from frying pans to heart valves—would have gone wanting.

If Plunkett had operated under the rules of should, he would only have been taken down the road of the also ran, where the crossroads of regret and lack of accomplishment meet. The rule on that sad journey says, among other things, "If you don't get what you bargained for, forget about it and move on."

This isn't to say that behaving according to should is wrong in every case. If you would like to experience every outcome should helps to create, then unwaveringly following should is fine. But not every should directed at you will be acceptable or in your best interest. At some point, as you become more and more aware of the purposes of should, you'll easily identify those who don't support you. They violate your sensibilities. If you're pushed too far, and certain people disrespect your desires one too many times, you may just have to assert yourself and give them a strong NO! Maybe even a scream might be in order.

This is where the difference between being accepting and lazy surfaces. For those accepting of things they dislike, whatever life presents is just fine. Cold weather and the furnace is broken? Great. No food? No problem. Hungry lions from the zoo escaped? Happy to have them!

But if the chilly weather, the empty plate, or the predators looking for prey bother you—and you don't do anything about them—the accepting person you see every morning in the mirror has slipped into another realm; the realm of the lazy. And doing something about that is well within your control.

The cure for laziness is to focus and press on toward your own cherished objectives.

13

A Rush to Understand

Helping people move on from wallowing in the muck and mire of situations to facilitating solutions is the best support you can offer.

Everyone has his or her own ideas about how things should be done, how life should be lived, and how everyone should interact with everyone else. The tendency to pass judgment is common. But, it isn't beneficial for long-term satisfaction, success, and achievement.

There are many ways this judging can emerge, but it's usually negative and critical. When it comes to evaluating people and their situations, judging tends to start out with two words: "I understand."

It indicates that you're convinced you have a pretty clear picture of the person and the problem—which may not be the case. Based on all the information you've been given, you might just have a-bit-better-than-vague idea of why this person is where he or she is at that particular moment.

When someone says, "I just lost my girlfriend (or boyfriend, job, truck, paycheck, or dog)," you know what he or she is talking about. You know this is more than just a hard-luck country/western song. And you may tend to assume the judge's robes with the simple phrase "I understand."

But as widespread as this judging business is, it's not terribly accurate, objective, or even fair. How can it be? Nobody totally knows what someone else is experiencing or all the nuances of the circumstances that led to that event.

There is always more to a situation than readily available information reveals. Even after a long explanation of how anyone got to where he or she is, critical elements are still left out. "Oh, yeah," the storyteller adds, "I thought there would have been a bridge there before we started to cross the canyon," which explains how she lost her boyfriend, truck, and dog!

But does the lack of complete information keep people from wanting to assume the judge's role, scratch their chins, and nod their heads in a way only experienced judges can? Absolutely not. The process of evaluation and decision-making has only just begun.

Sympathy Is a Negative Emotion—*Don't Go There!*

The next step is where the true effort at understanding and interacting either moves forward or falls apart. In too many cases, it collapses because the judge turns soft. Any benefit the person with the challenges might have had in sharing the information vanishes.

More often than not, the judge says "I'm sorry." The energy level then goes into the pits, and positive steps toward creating a solution are lost. The judge and the judged just sit there, wallowing in a bad situation that's made even worse by a mindset that says "Ohhh." Unfortunately, some people allow themselves to be forever stuck in it while holding on to the feeling that says "I'm a victim." Sympathy only makes things worse. The comforting phrase, "I'm sorry," doesn't encourage the person with the challenge to take positive action. Here's the difference between *sympathy* and *empathy*...

Sympathy says: "Ohhh. That's too bad. I'm sorry it happened. You poor baby." You crawl down into the hole with that person and throw a pity party.

Empathy says: "That's unfortunate. I know how you feel; I've been there myself and have felt the same way. But I'm stronger because of it and you can be too. This is an opportunity for you to grow. What are you going to do about it? What's your next step?" You throw a rope down to the person in the hole and say, "Grab a hold of it and I'll help you get out!"

So when the person with the unfortunate situation says, "I just lost my last four clients," which of these responses makes the most sense? Which response takes a significant step toward meeting the challenge and overcoming it?

Empathy, of course!

The only problem with this scenario—or any other in which someone needs a satisfying solution—is that the two questions, "What are you going to do about it?" and "What is your next step?" are rarely ever raised. This may seem too callous, too forward, or far too insensitive for most people to even consider—especially those who are stuck in their own quagmire of making excuses and not taking action.

By his or her own perspective, the person with the problem is in the middle of a catastrophe. So how is he or she supposed to know what the next step is and find the way out of the predicament? After all, according to the sympathetic point of view, that person is too busy being overwhelmed by the problem to find a solution.

Rather than just listening to people whine, encourage them to change their frame of reference—then notice the difference it makes. Helping people move away from wallowing in the muck and mire of situations and circumstances, to facilitating solutions, is the best support you can offer. It's the only way you can help others crawl out of the hole of self-pity and bring about positive change.

Empathy—*A Sweet Solution*

Imagine you're an investment banker. You're at your desk and one of your clients comes into the bank in a panic. It's Harry of *Big Harry's Ice Cream.* He has a great product. You've eaten Big Harry's high-calorie treats many times and they're really good. That's why you gave him the loan in the first place.

But there's a challenge now that the product's on the market. It seems, incredible flavors and all, that not everyone wants to sink his or her teeth into *Big Harry's Ice Cream.* Not everyone wants to take a big ol' lick of a Big Harry's mammoth ice cream cone. Sales are slow, and you say to Big Harry, "I understand."

And you DO understand. After all, you reviewed his business plan and cautiously handed Big Harry a check. Furthermore, you've talked repeatedly to him about his marketing and advertising campaign. "Harry," you said, at the time, "Ever think of changing your name to 'Tasty?'"

Big Harry laughed—shaking his 480 pounds like a bowlful of jelly. And now he has his face down on your desk, sobbing into his arm. "The ice cream," he blubbers. "It's not selling."

"I understand," you say. "SO, WHAT ARE YOU GOING TO DO ABOUT IT? WHAT'S YOUR NEXT STEP?"

In this case, these are business questions. Looks like it. Feels like it. Because the intent is to get the ice cream into people's hands—and stomachs—so Harry will sell his product and so you, Harry's banker, will not only get your investment back, but also make a profit.

How appropriate would "Oh, that's too bad" have been? How could sympathy possibly have helped? How could attending Harry's pity party possibly have supported him in overcoming his plight?

Look at sympathy in this context: It simply allows you to assess the situation, pat Harry's hand, say you feel sorry for him, and pontificate on just what he *should* have done. Sympathy is really no help at all, and judging becomes the alternative to action. This keeps both you and Harry stuck.

"Gee, Harry, you should have gone with another name," you would say. "It's too bad you made the choice you did. It's all terribly disappointing. My assistant will show you the door. Oh, one more thing, tomorrow's the first of the month and I'll be expecting a payment on your loan. Bye now."

Who wins here? No one!

You don't like the sound of that, and neither does Harry. So what if you're not Harry's marketing person? You have an investment in his operation, so it's in your best interest to encourage him to take some positive action.

Some people believe that sympathizing with someone is an end in and of itself. Of course, it doesn't demand anything of anyone—thought, action, or anything. It's also safe and inoffensive. But it's a lazy response to a clearly identifiable—and solvable—situation. And with each situation, there is virtually always a solution or a way out. It may not always be comfortable, but there's always a way.

Using empathy in working with someone to achieve an answer, isn't the same as should; not even close. Should keeps people stuck in the mindset of "I'm a victim," which leads to "If only…." It doesn't help them identify the next step that could be the beginning of momentum toward a very satisfactory solution.

Procrastination Can Lead to Seeking Instant Gratification

We all, at some level, have the innate ability to create our own solutions. Just go back a few thousand years when we were all fending for ourselves, either individually or in groups. Each of us had our own assignment; we understood through training how to execute our job, and we did it.

The challenge is that, as we've gone along through the years, too many of us have learned how *not* to cope. In our instant-gratification world, so much is done for us that many haven't developed the skills to succeed. As the generations have become more and more removed from the challenging, self-reliance-encouraging settings of centuries ago, many people, especially those of average thinking, do less and less and, as a result, become weaker and weaker.

Consider the case of poor Timmy. He wandered out of the house one day and, much to his chagrin, realized that a tire on his SUV had gone flat. It had been losing air steadily over the course of ten days. Every day for over a week, Timmy could have easily driven to one of the many local service garages and had the problem fixed. But he kept procrastinating and, finally, the only thing standing between the wheel rim and the street was a thin, squished layer of rubber. The tire was ruined.

Like most vehicles, Timmy's had a spare tire. But rather than getting out the jack and the spare, he called for help. He just stood around and waited. Within a half hour, sure enough, a rollback truck pulled up in front of the SUV, winched Timmy's vehicle up onto its floor, and drove off to a service garage to mount a new tire.

Timmy phoned his girlfriend for a ride to the garage and, after two hours of, again, just standing around, returned to the house in his flat-repaired SUV. Timmy hadn't lifted a finger. His wallet was significantly lighter, which he really couldn't afford, but he certainly didn't have to act on his own behalf. He was 27 years old, skied, camped, and hiked, but he couldn't or, more accurately, wouldn't change a tire. He thought he was above doing that sort of thing!

Of course, this scenario is good for the economy (the tow-truck driver and the service station), but it's bad for Timmy's financial situation. It reinforces procrastination and instant gratification as well as the idea that he can't do something when, in reality, he could.

So what happens the next time it looks like a challenge would develop? Even though Timmy knows he can handle it, he'll probably procrastinate until it becomes an emergency! He'll then call for help and pay dearly for someone else to repair the damage he could have prevented. He'll do what he thinks he should—just to look good. He isn't doing what he's *capable* of doing to save what little money he has. He doesn't understand doing it now or delayed gratification, and he's too lazy to do something that would increase his income! His behavior only serves to deepen his success-stealing habits.

Fortunately, not everyone procrastinates and is so willing to surrender to should. Many people take charge and use their resourcefulness every day. They expand sales territories, put together mergers, and do a hundred other positive things. They are responsible, forge ahead, and accomplish what they are fully capable of achieving. Not because they should, but because they made the conscious decision that this is what they want and they go for it.

To press on toward the life we want, many start their own business so they can go beyond just surviving to thriving. But for most people with a routine existence, the victorious feeling of even the survival aspect of life is missing. Perhaps this is why so-called reality TV shows are so popular.

Most people live a relatively safe life and aren't interested in taking the risks associated with climbing mountains, flying hang-gliders, rafting through white water, or spending weeks in environments where they rely on themselves to survive. Much of the world's population doesn't have to concern itself with basic survival. Today, keeping in touch with our survival skills requires more effort because of all the modern conveniences at our disposal. To make a masterpiece out of our life we need to cultivate our desires, while developing our skills and abilities. Pressing on toward your dream or objectives will provide you with the grandest adventure of all, causing you to stretch, grow, and become all you were meant to be. The people you meet and the new things you'll do in overcoming challenges along the way will add zest to your life.

> *"Life is either a daring adventure or nothing at all. Security does not exist in nature, nor do the children of men as a whole experience it. Avoiding danger is no safer in the long run than exposure to it."*
>
> —HELEN KELLER

All of those who have been thrust into change and not only survived, but chose to be better, stronger, and more loving because of it, have had to overcome obstacles. They called on themselves, marshaled their resources, asked for help as necessary, and moved ahead—often accomplishing more than they thought they could. They wanted to reach their goal or objective, and what others may have been inappropriately telling them they should or shouldn't do didn't hold them back from achieving it. They let go of those shoulds, ignored the naysayers, pressed on, and never looked back.

14

Magic Moments and New Paradigms

With each situation, there's always a solution, a way out. It may not always be comfortable, but there's always a way.

When I was nearly sixteen years old, I knew my life would soon change for the better. In the space of just one week, I would be a licensed driver. At least that was my goal. The results of the test, of course, would tell the tale.

Despite three months of practicing in parking lots and traveling back roads—with my sister in the seat next to me, prodding me on—and having mastered the clutch and the art of parallel parking, I was in a full-blown panic. I had read and reread the book of driving facts. I had memorized the road signs. I knew the minutia, down to who had the right-of-way among the four simultaneously arriving cars at a four-way stop. I was prepared yet, still, I was afraid.

On September 1st, I turned sixteen. By 9 a.m., I was at the licensing office having completed the paperwork, and passed the written part of the test. I was anxiously awaiting my turn for the gatekeeper—the man who would either grant me the privilege to drive, or keep me in driver's-permit limbo.

Ninety minutes later, it was done. I was driving a 1963 Corvair, a much overused car that had been branded by consumer advocate, Ralph Nader, as the most dangerous car on the road. These were mere details, easily overlooked by the fact that I now had a license to drive...by myself.

No longer would I have to find a willing chaperone to go with me. No longer would I have to coordinate with my mother's schedule, or make excuses to run an errand. I could just drive. The way I looked at the world—and how the world now looked back—had changed. At sixteen, I encountered one of life's significant paradigm shifts: from captivity to freedom. And nothing has been the same since.

In the overall scheme of things, getting a driver's license is a relatively minor accomplishment. It is nowhere near the order of ending a war, discovering the cure for a crippling disease, or landing on the moon. Nonetheless, each of these personal shifts changes the way we relate to the rest of the world and how they affect, to some degree, the way in which we live our lives.

But getting a driver's license, graduating from college, getting a job, getting married, or starting a business are as significant for the people involved as landmark achievements are for the discoverers or the peacemakers. Those smaller, personal achievements are brought about by the choices each of us makes for ourselves—to set a goal and reach an objective.

The Choice Reflex Leads to Taking *Productive* Action

Sometimes our actions are instant, subconscious, reflexive. We may be challenged by someone we're convinced is wrong, whose shoulds are delivered like so many jabs. But we respond verbally in a frank, firm, friendly, fair way, or through productive action, where before we may have just stood there and taken the abuse.

Other times, we ponder the challenge, examine it, analyze it, prioritize it, and rate its merits. We wrestle with it and, ultimately, decide what to do about it. A job becomes too demanding; the field of responsibility expands beyond every reasonable limit; the regular workweek jumps to sixty hours; or something else rears its ugly head into our comfortable world. We ask ourselves: "How did this happen? How is this influencing my family? How am I going to get my sanity back?" And then we do something.

Whatever the case, finding a quick resolution or taking a longer, deliberative path, it's the action—the productive action—that's critical. It's only by taking productive action, which is founded on our attitude, that we can get from where we are to where we want to be. Thinking and contemplating, studying and rehearsing are like the ritual preceding the driver's license. But they only prepare us to take productive action—the only element that can bring about change or accomplishment.

Now you might be thinking that simply acting doesn't assure success, and you'd be right. While picking up the phone to complain about a story reported in the newspaper is an action, it isn't an action that could influence the situation being written about. Going to seminars to learn how to build your business or career is only preparation for taking productive action. Productively applying what you learn is the only kind of action that will move you ahead.

Productive action involves exerting influence and energy to bring about change.

Author Stephen Covey discussed it in *The 7 Habits Of Highly Effective People*, when he wrote, "Almost every significant breakthrough in the field of scientific endeavor is first a break with tradition, with old ways of thinking, with old paradigms."

In this case, just remove the word scientific and substitute your own situation—the same dynamic applies. In social interaction, personal achievement, family growth, and business development, it's a break with tradition and old ways of thinking that will change your life. The break is critical, but it can only be facilitated by taking productive action. This is where, as they say, "The rubber meets the road."

The Red Flag of Should

At what point do we start to pay attention? At what point, between understanding the challenge and taking productive action, do we begin to notice more perceptively what is going on around us? When do we become more aware?

The first thing that typically gets our attention when something needs to be done is the imperative should. But far too often we accept should unthinkingly—either from others or ourselves—as the answer to our challenge.

Just as often, however, the advice that accompanies should doesn't fit. It doesn't apply to our situation, to our individual set of circumstances, or to our wants, needs, and desires. But it hangs in the air like a helium balloon, quietly bobbing at the end of a string, expecting us to automatically go along with it.

Start paying closer attention to your needs, the situations you face, and the solutions at your disposal, and you'll begin to more consciously lay the groundwork that will better enable you to take appropriate productive action.

Dealing effectively with should, in this case, begins with drawing a distinction between doing what you are told you should and doing what you believe is best. Analyzing the benefits of each is the challenge. Selecting one course or the other is the option. Taking appropriate productive action to achieve the best possible outcome, regardless of the shoulds thrown in your way, will enable you to thrive and prosper.

15

Establishing Some New Priorities

We all have challenges. They pay us visits dressed as everything from layoffs or being in a job we hate, to the sudden loss of a close friend or relative.

Not every opportunity to change direction is dressed in neon and broadcasted in surround sound. Not every crossroad is obvious. The opportunity for a break is often subtle, showing up as nothing more than a notion.

Here are five questions to ask yourself to help you determine if a paradigm shift is calling out to you, indicating a need to establish some new priorities. Answering them will help you put your new direction into perspective. You'll better be able to evaluate your core values and concerns, and draw a clean line between should and can.

- What is my most pressing challenge?
- What is my most urgent need?
- What is my most overwhelmingly strong desire?
- Where are my greatest responsibilities?
- Where would I find my most thorough fulfillment?

What is my most pressing challenge? We all have challenges. They pay us visits dressed as everything from layoffs or being in a job we hate, to the sudden loss of a close friend or relative. They're just a normal part of life.

But mixed among the challenges we overcome every day as they present themselves is one that stands out. It may be the one wedged between you and a friend or the next business or career. Identifying the situation and how you're going to deal with it can help you get on a completely different path.

What is my most urgent need? Needs are those things you can't do without. For example, address a need and you can continue to eat, breathe, or survive. Occasionally, our needs are threatened.

What need of yours is being ignored or stimied? How can you refocus on the person or thing that's calling for attention? How can you resurrect your interest in someone or something that once meant everything to you? Finding the answer may require an approach that is now completely foreign to you. Opening yourself to that possibility can make the quest itself an exciting reward.

What is my most overwhelmingly strong desire? An overwhelmingly strong desire is a want that won't go away, no matter how much you try to ignore it. The want for something often proves irresistible and can be the driving force behind many fine accomplishments. It drives people to perform feats that have run the gamut from being creative to seemingly crazy—and sometimes both.

What have you been denying yourself because you believed you weren't worthy or qualified? Too often, we convince ourselves that something is beyond us because we believe we don't measure up. In most cases, the only thing that needs adjusting is the way we look at the challenge of making it a reality and the approach we use to achieve it. Above all, start increasing your belief.

Where are my greatest obligations? We're social animals. We have relationships ranging from simple to complex, from next-door neighbors to siblings of in-laws, from one-time acquaintances to long-trusted allies. And our knowledge and respect for these people or groups is different.

Take time to focus on those with whom you are closest. The reason isn't that important. The feelings that draw you close to these people are what count. But, too often, we take people and relationships for granted. We lose touch with the emotions that make the alliance special. Find a way to reconnect with what you feel. For example, take your spouse out on a special date without the kids.

Where would I find my most thorough fulfillment? We can't find fulfillment without pressing on along our own path. One follows the other; they are inseparable. It's a symbiotic relationship. But too many of us go looking for the great feeling of winning without working to achieve what we claimed we wanted. We're left scratching our heads, thinking we've accomplished something, but muttering to ourselves, "Wait a minute."

Once you've identified when and where you're fulfilled, or the activity or person who helps fulfill you, you can recognize the path that will take you there. Sometimes changing the approach or adopting a new paradigm is the only way to achieve this. Sometimes, simply identifying and appreciating the thing or person who means the most is the only shift necessary.

When you begin to establish some new priorities and address the meaningful areas of your life, you can anticipate being rewarded with a sense of accomplishment. Begin to change with purpose and you can anticipate seeing the reverberations around you. Your results will change, your motivation will increase, and you'll impact others in a way that will bring them closer to you.

Address your core values and concerns, then what you need to change in your life will present itself. Your willingness to embrace the most effective shifts necessary will then become second nature.

16

Take Some Measured Steps

Surround yourself with positive, supportive people. They're the best antidote to the naysayers and shoulds nipping at you to give up.

Everyone has a dream. You may not have thought much about it for a while, or you may have simply lost track of it. But it's still there.

It's no secret why the desire we once dwelled on may now be nothing more than a misplaced memory. In many cases, we see the initial steps we need to take toward that objective. We may also know how we could best proceed in executing the plan and who could help us do it. We might even be able to see ourselves receiving the rewards of our efforts.

Unfortunately, we typically take a series of steps that move us in retreat. We run from taking positive actions and frantically scramble back to the old way. We opt for a route that inevitably takes us to a disappointing life. Sadly, we're left to examine what has just happened to us, shake our heads, and say, "I should have done it back then."

Just exactly what "it" is, is different for everyone. For example, "it" could be mountain climbing, owning a business or, perhaps, retiring from a job you no longer want to do.

The action you need to take is for you to decide. There's a choice to be made, and there's no shouldn't about it.

Here are 12 steps to goal setting—practical, systematic moves that will help usher you to where you want to go. They will help you put life's absolute commands in their proper perspective, whether the message comes from you or someone else.

1. ***Choose your goal.*** There are no shoulds when it comes to goals—they're different for everyone. For two high school friends aspiring to go to college, it probably won't be the same college. For new graduates, landing that dream job will likely take them in two different directions. For those with a job who are building a business to get free of it, the income it takes for freedom for one person is not the same as it is for another. For aspiring retirees, spending their golden years in the perfect environment can look as different as the deserts of Arizona, the mountains of Switzerland, or the coastline of Maine. Other people's shoulds have nothing to do with pressing on. It's entirely up to you.

2. ***Identify the benefits of reaching your goal.*** These could be spiritual, financial, educational, political, or something else—what motivates us is as individualized as our tastes in music or food. What you select as a reward for achieving your goal is entirely up to you. Just make sure it's attractive enough to keep you motivated. But don't let anyone tell you what it should be.

3. ***Visualize yourself with your goal met.*** You've achieved what you set out to do and now you're celebrating in the rewards. You're standing on the deck of your new home, holding a $1 million check to give to your favorite charity. Or perhaps you're savoring a political victory in the midst of reveling campaign workers. Is it enough? Is it what you an-

ticipated? Or is this reality check going to set you on your true course and save you from making a frustrating mistake? Is there another road that's better for you?

4. ***List the obstacles you need to overcome to reach your goal.*** Any military commander will tell you that a key to victory is anticipating what could happen during the campaign—the good and the bad. Knowing what is likely to *stand in your way* in pressing on toward your chosen objective will help you prepare for it and, with proper execution, avoid or overcome roadblocks, pitfalls, naysayers, and shoulds. But, of course, always be flexible to meet the unexpected challenges as well.

5. ***Identify groups and individuals you can work with to achieve your goal.*** Most of us have met enough cooperative people to know that we want to associate with those of *integrity* who have our best interests at heart—not *should*ers or naysayers. The papers that didn't get filed, the phone calls that didn't get made, or the report that didn't get written by the other person may have torpedoed repeated opportunities for success. So what can you do? Avoid people and live your life as a stoic loner? Not if you want to achieve *all* that you can, and make as big a difference as possible.

   The key is to select *smarter*. Take more time to interview or get to know those with whom you are considering associating. Are they naysayers or encouragers, positive or negative? When you're considering bringing people in to your sphere, be discerning, give them time to grow, and be sure to support them in pressing on.

6. ***Does it matter what skills and knowledge you need to reach your goal?*** This is one of the greatest opportunities for naysayers to stand up, laugh at your efforts, and send you scurrying for cover. If you're not careful, you could, once again, send your goal packing as you may have done before. Be committed enough to stick to it and do whatever it takes to reach it. Tell yourself to go for it.

If you don't believe you have the proper training or degree to press on toward your goal that doesn't matter. We often don't give ourselves the credit we deserve or we're too quick to discount the skills and knowledge we *do* have. Remember, the answer to "How?" is "Yes!" When your desire is strong enough, you'll learn how to achieve it as you go.

If a lack of confidence is holding you back from going for your goal, ask yourself this: What's the worst thing that could happen? Accept that as a possibility, and keep going!

7. ***Set a target date for reaching your goal.*** Knowing *where* you're going and *when* you're planning to arrive is standard practice for every successful endeavor, from taking a vacation to expanding a business. So why would it be any different for other personal and professional goals?

   Giving yourself a deadline will help you remain focused and help you measure your progress as you near the accomplishment. This isn't a should; it's a goal. If you don't reach it at the desired time, simply reset it until you accomplish it.

8. ***Write down your plan of action.*** Even people with the best memories forget something occasionally. Writing down how you are going to achieve your goal, and the specific steps you'll take to reach it, will cause you to focus. As you process it in your mind and put it on paper, it reinforces the tremendous power of intention which helps propel you to its completion.

   If need be, you may want some help in developing your plan from someone who has already accomplished what you're aiming toward. This plan will support you, step-by-step, in devoting your energies when and where you need them. You can then return to your overall goal, once those specific tasks are achieved, and determine what still needs to be done. Your action plan is a great safety net in pressing on, and can be adjusted as you negotiate life's twists and turns.

9. ***Reward yourself along the way for making progress.*** Who would take up a challenge that allowed them to celebrate

only what they'd accomplished five years later and *only* if they were maximally successful? Other than venture capitalists, who would invest large sums of money at great risk. Life is too short to live on the if-come. Enjoy the journey as you go. The process of pressing on in your own chosen direction *is* the success.

To put your nose to the grindstone and never look up as you go almost assures failure—or a huge collapse in interest. Taking a little time to recognize and celebrate your progress along the way will help you stay positive and focused and, ultimately, support and nurture you to even greater success.

10. ***Remind yourself of your goal daily, and structure your activities around reaching it.*** It's great to talk about having a goal. Millions of people do it every day. But how many actually pursue it? Far fewer. Why? It's often because they allow themselves to acquiesce to the naysayers and shoulds of everyday life.

    You've got a goal and you're pressing on toward it because of your passion, a sense of satisfaction and accomplishment, or a dozen other emotionally charged reasons. The key is posting your goal in words and pictures where you'll see it every day—on your refrigerator, bulletin board, by your desk, or elsewhere. Talking about your goal to those who love and support you is part of holding yourself accountable. But dedicating a portion of each day toward achieving your goal is the *only* thing that can lead to results.

    Your goal needs to be a part of your life—a passion. Otherwise, disappointment will surely come your way.

11. ***Remember to affirm your goal at least twice a day.*** For example, write down and say, "I'm financially free." This brief affirmation will help you stay on track. Say it enough, and you'll start believing it. Remembering why you're following the course you're on will help generate continuing enthusiasm for the project and assist you in establishing a network of people as you pursue its achievement.

12. ***Keep your eye on your goal, and watch out for old habits trying to sneak their way back into your life.*** The fastest way to avoid the pressure that a new behavior or goal introduces, as well as to thwart good work, is to forget about it and tell yourself you should go back to what you were doing before. At best, this is counterproductive. At worst, it's a self-defeating indictment of yourself.

    Once you've done considerable work to implement a new goal—one that you've been sacrificing for and celebrating as it has been developing—why would you go back to the old way? Because that's what others want? Because you should? What do *you* want?

Pressing on toward a new objective is a choice. Remember your frame of mind and the events that were swirling around you when you decided on this course of action. Surround yourself with positive supportive people and you'll have the best antidote to any naysayers and shoulds nipping at you to give up.

17

Speak Up for Yourself

If we say things without cooling off, thinking them through, our response often sounds hostile, cutting, and offensive.

Everyone deals with should in his or her own way. Some people turn quiet and sullen when confronted by it. They are the *sufferers.* They listen to what the *should*er has to say, blindly accept the advice without even considering their options, then simply do what they're told.

One step removed from the sufferers are the *plotters.* In nearly every case, they appear to casually accept the unsolicited should advice. But ignoring the *should*er is not what plotters are doing. Under their breath, under that exterior that seems to say, "Yeah, whatever," they are thinking a variety of things like: "How dare you!"; "Who do you think you are?"; "Be quiet!"; or "I'll *get* you!"

Plotters are either passive-aggressive (non-confrontational but angry) by nature, or perhaps previous confrontations have taught them to shut down and give up on their dream, much to their future regret. The plotters' failure to speak up for themselves in support of their own best interests can present itself in other ways. You may have observed this behavior before—in yourself or others—without being aware of it.

Here are three ways plotters try to cope with *should*ers, even though they don't give plotters the results they want:

- Selective listening. This occurs when the plotter hears only what he or she wants to hear and blocks out everything else the *should*er says, rather than speaking up.
- Purposeful forgetting. This is where certain communications from the *should*er seem to slip the plotter's mind when asked later by the *should*er.
- Destruction of objects. The plotter is so angry by what the *should*er said that he or she destroys something, like putting a fist through a wall. Afterward, the plotter maintains that it was purely accidental.

I mention sufferers and plotters and some of their behaviors because there are so many of them in the world, and their ineffective responses to should don't get them what they really want. Unless a should or a would or a shouldn't or a can't is dealt with directly, they might as well not respond at all.

> *Standing up for ourselves in the face of inappropriate shoulds is part of the commitment required so we can create the outcomes we want.*

Eliminate any Aggression—*If You Want Good Relationships*

Of course, the world isn't inhabited only by passive-aggressives. Others take on *should*ers with equal and opposite force. "I should dress up more often?" that person may ask in defiant reaction. "Well," he or she blurts out, "you should go for a long walk off a short pier more often! How about that, Buster? You aren't so perfect yourself. You should find a full-length mirror and take a long hard look at every inch, because you're the last person on earth who should be giving advice—especially on how to dress!"

And then there's the old standard: "You should take a flying leap!" While this expression falls in and out of favor, the sentiment often lingers just below the surface: "I'll tell *you* what to do, and we'll see how *you* like it!" is typically the message conveyed.

The unfortunate thing is that if we say things without cooling off and thinking them through, our response to the *should*er sounds hostile, cutting, and offensive. It's not the formula for success, happiness, or excellent relationships!

Unlike that of passive-aggressives, the confrontational approach has a major drawback. It drops an acceptably soft, unruffled exterior and revs up the engines of hostility like a sugar-addled, hypertensive kid without his or her medication. The upside to this kind of behavior is this: There is absolutely no question in anyone's mind as to what's going on and where you stand. Occasionally, this isn't such a bad thing. Most of the time, though, it's something to be avoided as it'll deteriorate your relationships.

Some of the telltale signs that indicate you are prone to giving passive-aggressive or simply aggressive responses to should and its variations include:

- Your first urge is to express anger in an effort to equalize the power imbalance the other person is trying to establish over you. The problem is, you'll only regret it later.
- You start to imagine how you would escape from the person trying to dominate you. But this won't help you grow.
- You imagine a new chapter in your life with this person where you never say another word to him or her. This is known as a "freeze out," but it doesn't help you deal with future challenges.

These examples reflect how people with passive-aggressive tendencies may think, and they're indicative of how they often respond when they're pushed too hard. Obviously, there are drawbacks. The recipients of passive-aggressive or aggressive responses may think you're unthinking, uncaring, or unappreciative of their "insightful advice." Or they'll simply brand you as someone who doesn't appreciate anything.

Of course—*you're a caring person!*

Remember that passive-aggressive and aggressive responses are acquired behaviors that can easily be kicked into action. There is little thought given to them because they may be so habitual. Employing them is often an unconscious choice.

If you decide to give an active response that's designed to shut a *should*er down and keep his or her shoulds from resurfacing, you need to be perfectly clear about his or her agenda. Freezing out the *should*er typically resolves nothing, and it could even encourage him or her in doing more *should*ing!

18

Lead the Discussion

Most people are fully capable of expressing themselves. This same capability can be transferred to responding when someone tries to sabotage us as we share our dreams.

Logic would tell most people that using should, shouldn't, or can't probably won't get them the results or attitude they want. However, few people are that logical or objective. If their manipulative ploys with should have gotten them what they wanted in the past with certain people who were weaker willed than they, they'll continue using should.

*Should*ers with successful *should*ing track records aren't likely to look at themselves objectively enough to change their approach without some kind of prompt. A short, simple message from you signals something is amiss, so the *should*er would do well to change his or her approach.

Here are some examples of how to do this:

- "That's an interesting idea, but I don't fully understand why you are suggesting it. Can you be more specific?"

  This allows you to interrupt the approach and get some kind of constructive dialogue going with the *should*er.

- "I'm not sure that would work for me, even though you seem convinced that this is the only way to go. Maybe you could explain why you feel so strongly."

  This puts the responsibility on the *should*er to explain him- or herself, and *may* help that person realize that what he or she is telling you is simply not acceptable.

- "I need to think about that. Can you give me more information about what you're proposing? I'll get back with you in an hour (or a day or so, or next week).

  This gives you the opportunity to assess what the *should*er is telling you, and how best to respond (not just react) to it. When you take away the pressure you might feel you have to give an immediate answer—one you may later regret—you also take away the urge to inappropriately express any potential anger.

Any one of these approaches will help defuse highly charged situations and assist you in making the best choice for you. Of course, you can avoid all of this interaction and cave in to the *should*er's demands by just saying "fine." But should isn't usually fine.

In negotiations, for instance, should is nothing more than an option. If you believe you should—if that truly holds some long-lasting advantage for you (not to just get the person off your back)—then great, do it. If it doesn't, dismiss it and move on.

In many cases, dismissing a suggestion is the most positive step you can take. It shows you are clear about what you *will* or *won't* do, while determining what *is* to your advantage and what *isn't*.

How to Talk with a *Should*er

If you decide to talk with a *should*er, there are some simple steps you can take to protect yourself. And you don't have to be a trained debater. Just use a little logic and say what's on your mind. Here are four steps you can take:

- Think about what's being said as it's being said.
- Be aware of the *should*er's emotional tone.
- Ask the *should*er to clarify what he or she is really asking for and why.
- Decline the *should*er's demand by using "I" in your response.

1. ***Think about what's being said as it's being said.*** Actually *listen* to the words coming out of the other person's mouth. Sometimes this can be a major challenge, especially when there are emotions involved. So take a deep breath, exhale, and then listen.

2. ***Be aware of the* should*er's emotional tone.*** This doesn't mean you have to focus on every harsh or cutting adjective. Just be aware of the fervor, anger, or sarcasm wrapped around the words. Then think to yourself, "This sounds an awful lot like my neighbor's crazy poodle!"

Now, would you yell at a dog simply because he's a little mixed up and barking at you? Probably not. Most of us, when we talk to dogs, use soothing tones and reason. The dog settles down, wags his tail, and the issue is resolved. But since you aren't dealing with a dog, you'll need to take the next step.

3. ***Ask the* should*er to clarify what he or she is really asking for and why.*** This is done using one of the examples detailed above and abbreviated below:

- "That's an interesting idea...."
- "I'm not sure that would work for me...."
- "I need to think about that...."

Requesting clarification from a should*er is a very powerful tool. It has the same effect as slamming on the brakes of a speeding, high-performance sports car.*

Even the most hard-charging, demanding *should*er is less powerful when he or she has to stop and restate his or her position, make it seem reasonable, or give you more information.

This can stop *shoulders* from continuing their charging-like-a-bull manipulative ways.

4. ***Decline the* shoulder*'s demand by using "I" in your response.*** This is easier than it sounds, and it can actually be fun. Simply say, "Herb (or Betty), that's not going to work for me because I…." and then fill in the blank.

For instance: "Herb! Being shot out of a cannon at the company's annual picnic isn't going to work for me: I'm afraid of heights, I'm allergic to gun powder, and it's not in my job description!"

Using I, me, or my in presenting your case is far less threatening that simply judging Herb and telling him, "You're crazy!" He'll be more inclined to understand your feelings, provided he's not put on the defensive, which saying "You're crazy" does instantly. Now you may think Herb's as crazy as your neighbor's poodle, but you don't have to tell him that. A little diplomacy can take you a long way toward getting what *you* want.

The Mediator's Approach

I've mediated many cases where people have been unable to agree—at least at the outset. As the bargaining process gets under way, Party A (the *shoulder*) will instruct Party B to behave like he or she should. If this happens, Party A reasons, things will be just fine. This compliance creates an outcome that enables Party A to walk away with a victory—whether it's deserved or not.

Mediations usually don't work out this way though. In most cases, coming to an agreement means a compromise where *both* sides get some of what each wants and needs. Should rarely plays a role. Remember, to help balance the discussion—ask the *shoulder* to elaborate on just exactly *what* he or she means and *why*.

There are other approaches that can also get *shoulders* to either make a more reasonable case or drop their demands. Party B can often achieve this outcome through:

- ***Active listening***: What I'm hearing you say is that I should always be willing to be shot out of a cannon.
- ***Reframing the statement***: When you say I should quietly walk away from the agreement, do you mean I should give you all the proceeds and take nothing for myself?
- ***Asking for clarification***: Just so I'm sure we are on the same page, do you mean I should never even mention my dream, let alone do anything to pursue it?

Any question or statement that gets the *should*er to reflect on what he or she is saying will help you slow the pace of the conversation and, possibly, encourage more reasonable thinking to prevail. It's generally not as if there are serious legal matters involved.

Typically, should statements focus on controlling someone else's behaviors, and managing discussions that relate to the actions needed to obtain certain outcomes. Most people are fully capable of expressing themselves when they're told they should dress formally rather than casually, or they should be wearing their hair up rather than down. This same capability can be transferred to responding when someone tries to sabotage us as we share our dreams. It just requires a bit more ingenuity, like using the examples presented above.

19

Show Your True Colors

Harness your emotions, responses, and interactions. Focus on and direct them, using them in an effective way that helps establish yourself as a person of influence.

All of us have things happen that we don't want or expect, such as:

- We enter into a relationship that comes up short on caring or sharing. Feeling let down, we think we've been taken unfair advantage of.
- We shake hands after an agreement. Two years after it was due we're *still* waiting for completion or delivery.
- We have a great dinner with two terrific friends. Next day we get a call from one telling us the other is no longer with us.

How you respond to any of these episodes speaks volumes about you, and puts your ability to interact with others in a valuable perspective. Especially when we talk about should, knowing how you tend to react and how you are capable of reacting will help in everything you do.

We all have our own response style to given situations. Sometimes our emotions present themselves as anger or sulking, handstands or laughter. Unfortunately, these emotion-driven responses aren't always appreciated by others. Some even dismiss them as inappropriate. Even though they may be entirely honest and spontaneous, others will frown upon them and, in many cases, tell you how you *should* feel and how you *should* respond.

Of course, these people are much more comfortable with flat emotions, measured responses, and stiff-upper-lip replies. This may be fine for them, but what about you? In their world of should, what *you* think is far down their list of concerns. But, of course, it's of primary concern to you. Harness your emotions, responses, and interactions. Focus on and direct them, using them in an effective way that helps establish you as a person of influence. Yes, unplanned-for things happen. But how you deal with them is the critical element. Giving appropriate responses allows you to engage others and create more of the outcomes you want. It gives you more control.

Reality Check-In—*Willingness, Ability, and Action*

There are three elements that can help you manage your responses and create the most desirable outcomes with others. These are your *willingness, ability,* and *action*, and they are especially important in dealing with should. Mentally walking yourself through these three phases will help you establish the outcomes you want, regardless of what others may have in mind for you.

First, let's look at Willingness. This deals with your will, your desire to do something, or the way you respond.

When someone says should, do you:

- Instantly do what is suggested without giving it any thought?
- Pause and let the directive sink in before you do what you're told?

- Listen to what the other person has to say before making up your mind about what to do next?

Exerting your will doesn't mean going into battle, with the more stubborn or bigger of the two of you getting his or her way. It's being willing to give yourself options. Life is full of choices, conscious or unconscious, and making the best ones possible is the first step in achieving your objective.

Next in this three-step approach is tapping into your Ability to overcome should and a host of other controlling directives. You may have all the will in the world, but unless you feel confident in pressing on along your *own* road to success—and have faith in the outcome it can produce—you're stuck.

What do you tell yourself when you examine your ability—that it's less than it should be, so you prevent the development of relationships? Or has it been so long since you exerted yourself that you don't remember what tapping into your ability feels like? Or do you tell yourself that you have faith in what you're doing and the direction you're headed, and that your ability just needs to be utilized?

Each of us has some level of ability to call on. We've all gone through school, relationships, jobs, and a myriad of other life challenges and dealt with them. Our ability to survive and thrive was called upon in every case. You're utilizing your ability and giving your *will* an opportunity.

Finally, in dealing with and managing should, there is Action. It's the final step in making your *will* real. Taking action is simply a matter of executing the choice—*your* choice—to press on and accomplish your goals. The next time you are challenged by should, ask yourself the following:

- ***What are my options to should?*** Responding with "What would I really like to do?" provides an initial barometer of the direction that will serve you best. Whether it's a short- or long-term goal, doing what is nurturing and rewarding for you and your family is best for your future happiness.

- ***What course is truly best for me?*** *What's best?* may be one of the most challenging questions we ever face. The final answer often doesn't come fast enough—especially when you consider that we live in a world where everything seems to come instantly: fast food, TV, the Internet, credit, tax returns, 6 a.m. Take the time to search your heart so you can honestly answer the question that'll help you take the most positive action. It's best to be away from the influence of anyone who's trying to should you into believing what they think is best for you.

- ***Am I WILLING to take the action to achieve what's important to me?*** Only you can answer this. You're the *only* one who has the true insight into your self-respect, character, conviction, and priorities. You're the only one who knows how you'll respond when shoulds or other obstacles come and you're faced with challenges that can send you into retreat.

- ***Do I have the ABILITY to achieve what I want?*** Look at the resources you have in place that will help you press on toward your objective. This typically comes in the form of personal conviction, skill, and training. Knowing what resources you have to draw on—and taking full advantage of them or, along the way, acquiring those you don't yet have—helps you build the confidence to move ahead. Once again, *the answer to "How?" is "Yes!"* You'll develop the ability as you go.

- ***If I need help to achieve what I want, where can I get it?*** Identifying networks of friends, associates, and other alliances, or establishing those you don't yet have, can make a huge difference in achieving what you want. You don't have to spend years acquiring every skill and bit of knowledge that will be needed. Associate with people who are where you want to be who can mentor you.

- ***What ACTION can I take—right now—to begin the process?*** The first step in pressing on is often the most important. Shed the shoulds and chart a course that will take you in the direction you want to go, then commit yourself to taking that first step *forward.* Put it in gear and get moving!

20

Stand Your Ground

Charting your own course and pressing on with a sense of self-assurance is the most liberating and empowering thing you can do for yourself.

It's a scene common to anyone who's ever shared his or her dream with negative-thinking people. They tell us we should leave things as they are instead of doing something new. They're convinced they know what's best for us, but it's just an excuse to maintain the status quo, founded on fear, ignorance, or a lack of faith.

For example, let's say you've recently started your own business. You share this with your friend Jack, with whom you've been bowling for a number of years. You tell him, that, unfortunately, you'll no longer be able to participate with the team because it conflicts with your new business activities. You confide in him that it's exciting and you see a lot of potential.

Jack quickly realizes that he'll be losing his star bowler, and goes into a long litany about how his Uncle Murray tried his hand at a business once and failed miserably. However, Jack fails to tell you that Uncle Murray wasn't committed to or excited about making his business a success like you are. After talking with a few naysaying *should*ers, Uncle Murray lost his dream, gave up, and begrudgingly chose to slog back and forth to a job he didn't like. He never made his business a priority like you're doing, and blamed being too busy with other things as his reason for quitting. But the truth is, he had taken his so-called business advice from people who weren't qualified to give it.

But Uncle Murray didn't tell the truth. He wasn't committed enough to stand his ground with the *should*ers and do what it took to make his business a success. He exhibited the losing behavior of not taking responsibility for pressing on toward what he claimed he wanted. He chose the self-defeating, not-following-your-own-path mistake of allowing status-quo *should*ers to influence him. He blamed others for his lack of results when, in reality, he had nobody but himself to blame. He gave in to the naysayers, excusing himself from pressing on. As a result, he's leading a lackluster life of sadness and regret.

The moment Jack shares this with you and stops talking, waiting for you to give in to his implied shouldn't, you have a choice to make. Do you straighten your spine, clear your head, and do exactly what's best for you, or acquiesce to his naysaying? This doesn't necessarily mean you put a determined look on your face, muster your courage, and shout the word NO—or maybe it does!

If you still need to consider what's best for you, remember, *best* refers specifically to course and *outcome*. If you continue with the scenario you're now involved in until it plays itself out, where will you be? What course and what result would be optimal for you? For example, is your current occupation giving you the life you want? Can it ever?

Stephen Covey speaks about leaning your ladder against the right wall. Put your energy in pressing on toward your own objective. The ladder is the path and the process of climbing it is your pressing on. The top of the wall represents what you want to achieve, how you want to live.

The same systematic approach will help you best in your efforts to deal effectively with should or shouldn't. When you hear the command, consider where following it would ultimately place you. Then immediately consider where you really want to be. If the spot you've *chosen* to aim for happens to be the same spot you've been told you should reach, that's terrific. Too often, though, it's not. Naysayers are known for criticizing people who are threatening to leave the box, trap, or status quo of familiar behavior.

Is It Wise to Consider Where Agreeing to Should Could Lead?

Ironically, there's a benefit to at least considering where agreeing to should could lead, even though it may be contradictory to what you have in mind. It can tell you where that person is in his or her thinking and whether he or she is a candidate to join *you* in *your* quest. It can be a catalyst to help you identify or reinforce the choice you've made and the result you're looking for. Your desire to move on only gets stronger.

We all stand our ground or acquiesce to should every day, often without realizing it. But those who easily give in, especially in areas that compromise their objective, rarely get what they want.

Determined, focused, stand-your-ground people never let naysaying *should*ers stop them from moving on. They consider the effect every action will have on their immediate and long-term plans as well as their relationship with the *should*ers. They reject the should or the shouldn't as politely as possible, and move forward doing what they need to do. They might say something like, "I appreciate your concern, but I know what I need to do for myself and my family."

Relationships, personal and professional, where some level of cooperation is desired or needed, often include compromising. That's where negotiating comes into play, sending two messages:

- You don't necessarily think that doing what you've been told you should or shouldn't do is best—*for you.*

- You're not necessarily going to *ignore* the other person, but it could be a savvy move in certain situations. If that person is obviously dedicated to dumping negativity on you and shows no regard for you or your desires, you may simply choose to ignore them! Associating with negative people only drags you down.

You might feel caught off guard and uncomfortable responding—at least immediately. You then tell the other person you need some time to consider what is being suggested, because you need to think about it—be it a few minutes, an hour, a day, or a week, depending on the importance or immediacy of taking action. When that time has passed, maintain integrity, either by getting back to the other person with your response or stating you need more time. Then think about it, discuss it with your spouse or leader/mentor, or whatever you need to do. Be aware that the other person may object to your need for more time. To this you can respond, "I really need more time to think about it and discuss it with.... It's simply too important." You've then pacified the other person and the situation, while buying more time for yourself. If that doesn't work, beware of being pressured by the *should*er.

Prepare a well-thought-out response to communicate your point. Practice it in front of a mirror or with a supportive audience: spouse, kids, a friendly stranger. This can help you make the best presentation of your response. It also helps you to be well-grounded emotionally, so the situation doesn't escalate out of control, especially if you believe you aren't in a very strong position.

Stop yourself, bolster your resolve, and proceed to make your point in a kind but firm way. This organizational period will help you focus on your goals and decide what may be negotiable—what is open for discussion and compromise and what isn't. This step-by-step approach is most effective in clarifying what's important to *you,* so you can communicate effectively.

The Exception to *The Rule*

Should is only a word, but words have built and lost fortunes, and started and stopped wars. They are powerful tools to help you accomplish what *you* have decided is important.

When you hear should relative to some objective, you'll know immediately if it's meant in a positive or negative way. Was it to build you up or tear you down; to build a fortune or start a war; to keep you stuck or encourage you to press on?

In most cases, should is used as a negative controlling tool used to influence you to act in someone else's best interest but not your own. Even if there's no financial gain to the *should*er, simply knowing you've been influenced to act in a certain way is payoff enough. He or she may be looking to gain some sort of control in what may be an out-of-control life. This short-term satisfaction legitimizes should in that person's mind. It worked before, so why not use it again?

In a small fraction of cases, should can be an asset. It can be used as a tool to reinforce what's best for you. "You should always follow your dream and stick to your values" is advice from someone who has your best interest at heart. Perhaps he or she will add, "How can I help?" Now that's a person to associate with and learn from!

But the tone and intent quickly changes when should is used in its typical, manipulative form: "You should go to this school," "You should take that job," "You should stay at home rather than go out and build a business," "What's this dream stuff? You should just be thankful for what you have." These are all undermining commands. While they may appear to be in your best interest, they are meant to rob you of control over your future and thinking for yourself.

The difference between a should that benefits you and a should that just benefits the *should*er is usually obvious. If you have an immediate stomped-on feeling because you've just allowed someone to rob you of a choice and the power to control your own destiny, the advice isn't in your best interest. It's meant to thwart your efforts rather than applaud and support them.

Could the Should Be Legitimate?

If there is any question about the sincerity and intent of the advice giver, take a few minutes and go down The Should Legitimacy Checklist. Take these steps if you believe there might be some advantage in following what the *should*er has suggested, and you want to be more sure of that person's agenda.

1. Do you respect anyone who tells you what you should be doing? Is he or she where you want to be? What's your relationship with them? What led to the relationship in the first place? What is it built on? Is it just an habitual association you have long outgrown?

2. Has he or she been right or nurturing in the advice given to you in the past? Look at those earlier outcomes. If you've followed his or her suggestions before, have the outcomes been positive or negative?

3. What's this person's *motive* and how is he or she going to benefit by having you do what's suggested? Only when your best interest is involved and you benefit, too, are you to even consider this advice.

4. Finally, ask yourself, "Does this make sense given the direction I want to go in?" An honest, rational reply will help you decide what course to take.

If acting on this person's previous advice has been a benefit to you, you might want to consider taking it again. If the record has been marred with false starts, broken promises, and disappointing ends, then run—as fast as you can—in the other direction!

Look at *The Motive*

People form and maintain relationships for a variety of reasons, from family ties to addressing neighborhood concerns and initiating kids' activities—as well as getting things done on the job or in business. Changing relationships—for whatever reason—creates its own set of challenges, from hurt feelings to misunderstandings or blame. Sometimes people just get too lazy to step away from a controlling or otherwise difficult relationship. But as we grow and change our thinking, then move in a direction that leads us to the achievements we desire, it is inevitable that certain outgrown relationships have to go. The great thing about this is that it makes room for new people who will befriend and support us.

More often than not, those old relationships include advice giving which, if followed, lead to being stuck rather than working toward a better life. Should inevitably jumps to the forefront of the conversation. It's easy to do, assumes little or no responsibility or risk for the outcome, and gives control to the *should*er.

A friend of mine, I'll call her Mary, admitted she likes a sense of power. She noted that it's much easier to give advice to others—with the unblinking expectation that they'll follow it—than it is for her to follow her own advice.

The conversation that day was about food—on which Mary is an expert. She has read all the books on nutrition. She knows every vitamin and molecule that makes up every shred of consumable matter in any given meal on earth. Mary has a wealth of knowledge, and she is more than willing to share it with anyone who will listen, too slow to walk away, or too polite to say "That's enough."

The ironic part of this story is that much of Mary's advice centers on calories. She carefully, thoughtfully, almost fanatically explains that what her dinner partner is putting into his or her mouth isn't necessarily what should be put in there.

Mary confides, "Weight can kill ya. Knew you'd want to know."

The irony leaps into the equation when you look at Mary. She crossed the line into the 300-pound territory a long time ago. While she may not be happy at that weight, she continues living there. And from that perspective, as ironic as it is, Mary attempts to control everyone but herself.

Mary isn't alone.

People preach everyday on how to live a clean, healthy, moral life, but would never do more than think fleetingly about pressing on themselves. They make plenty of excuses: It's too hard. It's no fun. It's not what *everyone else* is doing. So they don't either. But that doesn't keep them from whispering in your ear how you should be living your life.

It's easy to tell others what they should do, and it's nearly as easy to comply with others' shoulds. This is especially so when should comes from someone who is strong and usually correct in his or her thinking. But just consider should as input that is to be accepted or rejected, depending on its relevancy to your objective. You retain the decision-making and the growth opportunity of thinking for yourself. It's part of leadership. It stirs things up, but think about it. Nothing changes if things aren't in flux!

To be a leader, rather than just a passive recipient in life, requires taking more responsibility. This is challenging, but charting your own course with a sense of self-assurance is the most liberating and empowering thing you can do for yourself. You are taking the bull by the horns, so to speak, rather than letting the life you want pass you by and regretting it later.

Invest in Your *Own* Desired Outcomes

Managing shoulds more effectively helps you go to a new level in your thinking and, therefore, your success. Increase your faith and believe in your new objective and in what you're telling yourself and others about it. You'll occasionally run the risk of others reacting negatively to you, but that's okay. They may even try to further manipulate you by a display of hurt feelings, misunderstandings, or resentment. Few people like disagreements, but for progress to be made, it's often necessary. Saying things that support where you are headed, to which people may respond unkindly, isn't the solution in and of itself. The risk of receiving negative responses from people who see you as shaking up the status quo is simply par for the change process.

Consider this: What if more people would be willing to lay down conditions for relationships that support both party's objectives. Isn't that the ultimate win-win? Wouldn't this, alone, keep negativity to a minimum? It's not healthy to keep dissent bottled up inside until it can be contained no more. But it has become such a habit that most people don't even consider that this is what they're doing. They have always let people take them off track because their commitment simply wasn't strong enough.

People, in their efforts to avoid rejection, give in to others who don't really care very much, or at all, about them. Facing this can be uncomfortable. But, the true test of a relationship comes when one person chooses to change the norm by taking a different track. How does the one person respond who professes to love or at least care about the other? How selfish or caring is that response? Rejection is part of the risk everyone takes when sharing what's truly on his or her heart, and begins to act on their new priorities. But rejection always provides a new opportunity.

Let's look at how focused, committed, and practical we can be when we're pressing on. Look at the investment you've made in your business or career so far. You knew going in that it would take six months to get a realtor's license, a year to build the foundation for a good business, four years for a bachelor's degree, or half a lifetime to finally practice comfortably as a medical doctor. You had to devote hours to studying, probably lived within a budget, made sacrifices, and executed your plan. This saved you from some surprises and disappointments, and allowed you to live your life with basic control and perspective.

We Become Like the Company We Keep

Take similar steps when it comes to establishing and maintaining positive relationships and letting go of negative ones. Remember, we become like the company we keep. Invest time evaluating people, their behaviors and shoulds, and your desired outcomes. Intelligently relate to others so you can create the life you want.

Practice this evaluative behavior and encourage it in others. Such a thoughtful approach is one of the most loving things we can do for ourselves and others. Simply consider what's happening when someone tries to dissuade you from the objective you know is best, and press on in spite of any fears you may have. If you don't, you'll only live to regret it.

With this new perspective, you no longer allow others to dictate your behavior. With your new level of awareness and a renewed commitment to your objective, no one can cause you to lose your way. If you inappropriately please others by forgetting about your desires, your level of discontent will only increase.

Your commitment to your objective propels you to analyze relationships. Consider a challenging situation where you studied some confused interaction and successfully sorted it out. Look back on that and continue being aware of how your relationships are affecting you and your quest. It's the right thing to do—for everyone concerned. Be as kind and compassionate as possible while standing your ground. It's part of moving forward while holding yourself and others accountable.

Improving your should-challenging skills takes some effort. It requires some mental and emotional stretching—maybe a lot. But once you've set up a system of responding to others who are trying to control you, effective responses will become second nature.

Increased commitment and excitement will be two of the payoffs. You'll also improve your relationships as you rediscover a firmer foundation where your life is in balance and virtually anything is possible. It leads to a happier, more satisfying, smoother-running life.

21

Build Better Relationships and Lead More Effectively

*As you progress, you can teach and lead others by the example of your non-threatening, no-*should*ing approach.*

Should has become so widespread that it's nearly impossible for many people to have conversations without using it. Not using should may cause long pauses while we look for reasonable alternative words to lead people without manipulation. That's okay, since...

> *...alternatives to should are more likely to lead to understanding,, consensus, and cooperation.*

Imagine a world that operates with these concepts. Thinking and speaking in alternative terms allows you and everyone else involved in the conversation to create a more compassionate atmosphere, where people will want to be and do more, and anything is possible. Here are twelve examples for doing so, while leading others to do what you'd like them to do:

1. ***Conceivable?*** *Would it be conceivable for you to rearrange the work schedules the first weekend in March so I can have it off to do something special with my wife?* This approach is far more likely to get the boss to go along with you than telling him he *should* rearrange the work schedule! The conceivable questioning approach increases the chances that the person on the receiving end will accept it, without feeling pressured to act in a specific or controlled way.

2. ***Just Imagine.*** *Just imagine how your life will be when you can do whatever you want.* Once you employ the imagination, yours or anyone else's, anything is possible. *Should* dictates only one way, but calling on the imagination helps get people dreaming.

3. ***Legal, moral, and ethical.*** *It's legal, moral, and ethical and done by many wonderful people.* This puts people at ease as it implies it is widely practiced by good people, conveying the message that the idea falls within accepted societal norms. You're more apt to have a positive influence on someone than you would if you said that person *should* do it.

4. ***Emotion and logic.*** *Most people make decisions based on emotion backed up by logic.* Sharing what you would like someone to do—with emotion—and giving them the logic behind the idea will get far better results than telling them they *should* do something.

5. ***It may be.*** *It may be a good idea for you to do it.* This provides a solution without trying to should the person into doing it. It gives them something positive to think about and a direction in which to proceed. They won't feel pressured.

6. ***Potential.*** *Doing what you're suggesting offers the listener the potential of accomplishing a goal.* This communicates that there's a benefit in doing what you'd like the listener to do. Trying to *should* the listener into doing what you want would only alienate him or her.

7. ***Possibilities.*** *The possibilities are endless.* What would the future be like without possibilities? Telling someone something is possible gives them hope. It can get them thinking in your direction and taking action, whereas should would shut them down.

8. ***If not this, what?*** *Asking this can get the listener moving in your direction.* It can cause the listener to realize they probably don't have any better alternatives or offers. They may start believing that if they don't do what you're suggesting they'll lose out.

9. ***Reasonable.*** *It's probably the most reasonable thing to do.* Most people think they are reasonable. *Reasonable* implies that you have the ability to process information correctly and select the best choice for all concerned. The listener is more likely to follow your suggestions, where *should* would cause him or her to be repulsed.

10. ***Sensible.*** *I'd like to share this with you because it makes a lot of sense.* This is music to the ears of linear thinkers and those who think they have a lot of common sense. *Sensible* helps even the scattered to start believing in themselves and your proposal for them to take action.

11. ***Sound.*** *It's a sound investment or opportunity.* Sound is used by bankers and dads in a moment of meaningful reflection. Whenever something is presented as sound, it infers that it is well thought out and, therefore, the right thing to do. Tell someone it's an investment or opportunity he or she *should* take advantage of, and they'll probably shy away from it.

12. ***Could.*** *You could do it, that is, if you really want the results you talked about.* This does not interfere with the person's right to make a choice, while providing him or her with an incentive to do what you know is in their best interest—as well as yours. The listener doing what you propose can lead him or her to creating a result desired by both of you. If you

were to tell the listener he or she *should* do it, they're likely to feel pressured and not do it!

Of course, there are other alternatives to should that can help people get inspired to perform in positive ways. Using should alternatives is the least you can do when you're committed to using your time and energy wisely in pressing on. As you progress, you can teach and lead others by the example of your nonthreatening, no-*should*ing approach.

22

The Voice of Cyberspace

Pressing on elevates us from just surviving in what may be a status-quo world of frustration and limits, to living a happier, more fulfilling life built on pursuing objectives and making dreams come true.

Some people assume that all the information they find on the Internet is honest, well-intentioned, and correct, and take it as the gospel truth. This is most unfortunate. As great a tool as the Internet is, it's also loaded with a lot of hearsay, innuendo, outright lies, and sour grapes. Just as in person, there are a lot of whiners and complainers on the Internet who try to dissuade others from pressing on. Yes, believe it or not, jealousy is alive and well on the Internet, just as it is in real life.

To put the search for easy, "authoritative" information into some perspective, it's important to understand how many people are invested in using the Internet. As you might suspect, the United States leads the way, followed by China, Japan, Germany, and India. The total worldwide is over 1.2 billion!

Of course, this number was generated through an Internet search. In the minds of many, the number is above reproach. After all, it came from online.

But how reliable is it? How reliable, authoritative, or accurate is any information when the pool of hits for one search term generates millions of responses, based on thousands of interpretations of just what exactly is being asked? How can they help you press on, now really?

Take the example of "entrepreneur." The Google definition seems pretty straightforward: "A person who organizes, operates, and assumes the risk for a business venture."

And then we're off to the Google races with about 38,800,000 "results."

So where do you go from there? More importantly when you get down to, say, result number 3,219,485, do you really trust the information, especially when an entrepreneurial person is characterized as the following?

- Having lots of ideas but can't focus and runs in circles.
- Not good with details.
- Feeling odd, different, alone, strange.
- Good at starting businesses, but bad at running them.
- One who perpetuates chaos, which reigns in their company.

In the interest of full disclosure, this list was in an article by a business coach. This individual's motivation for casting our hypothetical small businessperson in such a dim, peculiar, disparaging light is biased and more than a little self-serving. After all, this person who calls himself a coach is supposedly here to help entrepreneurs, not discourage them.

If you didn't give the result at least a little critical thought, and wonder what this so-called coach's agenda is, you might well assume that all entrepreneurs can't focus, aren't good with details, are a little strange, and they can't really run their businesses very well because, well, chaos reigns. If that were true, rather than an embittered, cynical, sour-grapes view, we could still be in the caveman's developmental day!

But there it is, clear as day, on the computer screen—the authoritative voice of the Internet. But does *that* make it true?

Some other perspectives from the millions-deep Internet entrepreneurial pool hint at the breadth, if not the width, of what lingers in cyberspace:

- "Entrepreneurs often act as lighthouses in workplaces marked by unrelenting consumerism and desperate lives. But what defines this successful innovator's brain?"
- "Approximately 10.1 million adults in the U.S. are attempting to create a new business at any given time. With nearly one half of all new ventures started by teams of people, this represents about 5.6 million potential new businesses."
- "So you want to be a hi-tech entrepreneur? Oh, it's a huge pain...."

How Can We Make Sense of All the Information on the Internet?

This brings us back to the original point: How do you make sense of the avalanche of so-called information on the Internet, and what sources can you honestly trust?

First, the avalanche issue: Obviously, no one has the time or the attention span to cull through 38,800,000 results. Of course, at this point you would refine the search and probably get the number down to 12,000 or so. But this doesn't really do much to address the time/attention challenge. After all, 12,000 is still much more than overload. What if there are several hundred takes on the same subject, which there are likely to be? Then what?

The first thing you might want to consider is disempowering the Internet and only seeking out quality advice from people with real expertise—people you can trust. This allows you to establish relationships with people who actually know a great deal about how you can best press on—real people who are qualified to give you advice!

These people can also answer direct questions and not offer 38 million options. If they don't have the answers to your specific questions, in all likelihood they can refer you to someone in their trusted network or sphere of influence who can be of help.

Expanding your network through the proven networks of others can do several things: give you additional insight, allow you to actually talk with live human beings (rather than your computer), and develop your own networks for whatever purpose you choose later on.

This is not a suggestion to ignore the Internet or the services it offers. It can be a great tool, but it can't build an interpersonal relationship with you or care about you.

More Elements and Hazards of Going Online for Advice

1. **Email**—Let's be honest. How many times a day do you check your email? Once, twice, 38,800,000 times?

Like the Internet itself, email can be of great benefit if used in moderation. But it's also a source of aggravation because of overuse, misuse, and abuse. In the process, it often proves to be another great waster of time. Consider the usual email suspects:

> ***Spam***—While most Internet service providers offer spam (unwanted, unsolicited email) blocks, that doesn't assure that this email advertising won't make it to your in-box. Of course, the natural inclination is to delete any messages that have a return address you don't recognize. But there can be drawbacks to this approach: you may end up deleting messages that could have benefited you.

> ***Forward***—This can be one of the most maddening, guilt-causing wasters of time in the world. These are inevitably sent by people you know who, gauging by the abundance and length of their messages, have entirely too much time on their hands. While the inclination may be there to delete, delete, delete, one of those messages may carry an original message you would have liked to read.

2. **Shopping & Planning**—What better way to find that perfect something you don't yet realize you need? Or how about

planning that trip, booking the hotel and car, and pre-touring every tourist attraction within 500 miles of your destination? Imagine chewing up hour after hour of what could be productive time! This is not good.

3. **Chat**—Who doesn't like to talk and keep their "friends" abreast of all the latest developments, everywhere? The Internet provides us with instant access to: "chat rooms for teens, kids, singles, and more"; "family-oriented chat environment, staffed by trained administrators; "understanding and overcoming the grief of losing at love"; "details of every part of any country, their music, genealogy, and more," etc., etc. in ad nauseum.

The Internet is great for executing all of the above activities. The disconnect comes when these activities turn into obsessions, and real work and achievements are sacrificed. At this point, the Internet becomes one of the most serious distractions and wasters of time ever devised by man.

Of course, most business owners don't have the patience to spend more than two minutes away from their core business. The incessant use of the Internet, email and chatting, especially chatting, constitutes little more than time thieves.

To most effectively guard against the abuse, over-use, or intimidation of the Internet in running your business and personal activities…

- **Take it for what it's worth**—Results from an Internet search don't translate into an equal number of leads—not even close. Many of the sources are spouting off, pontificating.

- **Use it as a tool**—The Internet can help you generate some ideas or give you additional insights. But you need to start with a strong base, an understanding of who you are, and a clear sense of your professional and personal objectives.

- **Know what's important**—There are a number of popular sites that get huge amounts of publicity, but most of what those sites carry have nothing to do with running a successful career, business, or life. They take your focus off *your* objectives.

- **Don't get distracted**—Diversions are everywhere. The Internet can be one of the biggest distractions if you allow it to consume your time. Remember, it's not your friend, confidant, parent, mentor, leader, or other important player in your life. If it becomes something more, your success and happiness in business and in life will probably suffer.

Epilogue

Are You *Really* Pressing On Toward YOUR Objectives?

Don't let others run your life, either online or off. Appropriately responding to those who would love to have control over you is key for you to press on.

Are you pressing on toward *your* objectives? It's a question everyone would like to respond to with an emphatic "YES, I AM!" But are you *really*? Or are you letting others, even hearsay on the Internet, affect what you do?

Some of the people we know may do some bidding for our time and energy, while others might even demand control. Their approaches are limited only by their ingenuity in making requests, giving advice, or issuing commands. But the great thing is, you have just learned the basics of how to identify and appropriately deal with the *should*ers among them. You are now equipped with some powerful new tools with which you can build a better tomorrow and help others do the same!

Skillfully responding to should and other potentially controlling or discouraging words is of utmost importance. It helps us claim the power to press on. Doing so elevates us from just surviving in the status-quo world of boredom, frustration, and limits, to living a happier, more fulfilling life built on self-assurance and making dreams come true. You can now more effectively deal with any situations that threaten to take you off course—by using what you have learned in this book.

Eliminating any confusion, making up your own mind, and taking positive action is the most effective strategy in dealing with those who would try to get you off track. Kindly, but firmly, putting them in their rightful place empowers you to create the life you really want.

Naysayers either in person or online, can no longer daunt you or direct the course of your life. Hearsay, negativity, or innuendo, whether found on the Internet or from other sources, can no longer keep you from pressing on.

Respond with purpose and meaning, especially in your heart where it counts the most, to those whose agendas are not in your best interest—and move on. That offers a clear sign to yourself, as well as to those who would otherwise try to control your life. Sooner or later, they'll realize their efforts are futile and your resolve will have won the day. This is the only way you can ever hope to continue pressing on—with greater commitment than ever before.

The answer to "Are You *Really* Pressing On?" is now perfectly clear. There's no doubt about it. The answer is "YES, I AM!" You're ready, willing, and able. Now let's *press on.* Make it happen!

Who Is Michael Kerrigan?

Michael Kerrigan is a motivational speaker and mediator, and the president and founder of LifeTime Services, which creates life-skills programs and training materials for young people and adults.

His first book, *What Choice Do I Have?* is a popular guide to help people make better choices that can empower them to better direct their lives so they can achieve what they want. Michael has also developed audio programs that focus on change, choice making, maximizing potential, and relationship building. For children, he created a self-paced course focused on personal development and responsible behavior, as well as a curriculum on negotiation.

Michael worked as an investigative reporter and national correspondent, having spent more than a decade with newspapers and magazines across the U.S. He lives in Colorado.